500 TABLES

500 TABLES

INSPIRING INTERPRETATIONS OF
FUNCTION AND STYLE

LARK BOOKS

A Division of
Sterling Publishing Co., Inc.
New York / London

SENIOR EDITOR
Ray Hemachandra

EDITOR
Julie Hale

ART DIRECTOR
Jackie Kerr

COVER DESIGNER
Jackie Kerr

FRONT COVER
Adrien Rutigliano Segal
*Tidal Datum Tables, Verified Water Level:
San Francisco, CA 2006/04/27-2006/05/24,*
2007

BACK COVER, FROM TOP RIGHT
Garry Knox Bennett
Hall Table and Chair #2, 2006

Chris Bowman
Hey Series #1, 2006

Michael Gloor
Bot Table, 2005

Fred Baier
Tetrahedron and Torroid Table, 1995

SPINE
Graham Campbell
Luricka, 2002

FRONT FLAP
Patrick L. Dougherty
Cosmos Table, 2007

BACK FLAP
Kerry Vesper
Altar Table, 2004

PAGE 3
Floyd Gompf
Homage to FLW: Coffee Table, 2005

PAGE 5
Jeff Wallin
Tsunami Table, 2006

Library of Congress Cataloging-in-Publication Data

500 tables : inspiring interpretations of function and style /
senior editor, Ray Hemachandra ; editor, Julie Hale. — 1st ed.
     p. cm.
  Includes index.
  ISBN 978-1-60059-057-3 (pb-pbk. with flaps : alk. paper)
  1. Tables—History—21st century—Catalogs. 2. Studio furniture—History—
21st century—Catalogs. I. Hemachandra, Ray. II. Hale, Julie. III.
Title: Five hundred tables.
NK2740.A17 2009
641'.5—dc22

2008032589

10 9 8 7 6 5 4 3 2 1
First Edition

Published by Lark Books, A Division of
Sterling Publishing Co., Inc.
387 Park Avenue South, New York, NY 10016

Text © 2009, Lark Books
Photography © 2009, Artist/Photographer

Distributed in Canada by Sterling Publishing, c/o Canadian Manda Group,
165 Dufferin Street, Toronto, Ontario, Canada M6K 3H6

Distributed in the United Kingdom by GMC Distribution Services, Castle Place,
166 High Street, Lewes, East Sussex, England BN7 1XU

Distributed in Australia by Capricorn Link (Australia) Pty Ltd., P.O. Box 704,
Windsor, NSW 2756 Australia

If you have questions or comments about this book, please contact:
Lark Books, 67 Broadway, Asheville, NC 28801, 828-253-0467

Manufactured in China

ISBN 13: 978-1-60059-057-3

For information about custom editions, special sales, and premium and corporate
purchases, please contact the Sterling Special Sales Department at 800-805-5489
or specialsales@sterlingpub.com.

Contents

Introduction by Ray Hemachandra **6**

The Tables **8**

About the Juror **414**

Acknowledgments **414**

Contributing Artists **415**

Introduction

The furniture presented in this book showcases a fantastic diversity of styles and materials, with an impressive array of continents of origin and intended uses. Objects like tables tell us a lot about their makers and designers. What interests them philosophically? Historically? Artistically? As you flip through these pages, try to imagine a bit about the maker of a table that is just barely functional but exquisitely made. Or, speculate where a maker first saw that 18th-century card table he or she is reproducing: Is it a true and perfect reproduction, or some subtle twist on the original, reflecting an ironic sense of humor? Sometimes teasing out an answer can be difficult, which makes trying to figure out a table all the more fun!

As the Executive Director of the American Craft Council and former Executive Director of The Furniture Society, juror Andrew Glasgow has spent countless hours over the years in conversation about, looking at, sitting in, sleeping on, writing at, eating on, and interacting with studio furniture. His goal in making selections for this book was to feature a wide variety of work while demonstrating the highest quality of furniture making. He brought to the jurying process his years of experience looking at thousands of pieces of furniture; he knows how to assess when materials and design are working in tandem, when proportion is correct, and when to say "no thanks," especially when a piece lacks clear overall identity from a design, material, or use perspective. The tables presented in this volume cover a terrific spectrum of possibilities, and I hope you'll agree with most of the choices from an artistic standpoint. But when you don't, I also hope you'll try to figure out why Andrew made the decision to include a particular table.

Floyd Gompf
Wheeled Side Table | 2007

One of the issues that arises most frequently in the studio-furniture community has to do with contemporary design versus traditional design. The sharp tensions between these approaches keep work and perspectives fresh. This book celebrates both the sculptural innovation and the careful attention to historic detail that makers bring to their craft. There's more than enough room for both approaches in the modern furniture-making world. And rest assured: Examples of outrageousness—both bold experimentation in sculpture-based furniture design and striking plays off of traditional design and construction techniques—will greet you throughout this volume. The range of work is simply dazzling, reflecting the extraordinary skills of modern furniture makers.

Mark S. Levin
*Pear Coffee Table
with Drawer* | 2007

Many designers use whimsicality as the foundation for inventive pieces. *Clothespin Table* by Mervyn L. Krivoshein (page 164), *Pear Coffee Table with Drawer* by Mark S. Levin (bottom left), and *Get Some Zs* by Kevin J. Waddell (opposite page) are clever reconfigurations of traditional tables that demonstrate a wonderfully fanciful aesthetic. This same sort of playfulness is evident in tables that feature unconventional design elements. Making ingenious use of found objects and recycled items, Floyd Gompf's *Wheeled Side Table* (top left), Greg Gehner's *Tongue and Groove End Table* (page 254), and Steven T. Samson's *African Nail Fetish Coffee Table* (page 11) are cunningly conceived pieces that transcend the standard definitions of table.

In addition to these witty, innovative pieces, you'll find minimalistic creations—tables marked by an economy of design created by artists who know how to make bold statements with simple forms and modest materials. Richard Judd's clean, uncomplicated *Bird Table* (page 17), John Makepeace's dramatic *Wave* (right), and Kino Guérin's beautifully fluid *Estrella Table* (page 30) exhibit a scaled-back elegance—a spareness that's cool and contemporary. Standing in contrast to these minimalistic pieces are tables that call attention to the design process through complexity of construction. Janice C. Smith's *Honey* (page 226), Steve A. Butler's *Sherwood—Coffee Table* (page 348), and Matthew Wellman's *Shaker Table, Exploded View* (page 283) are intricately assembled pieces that seem intentionally architectural.

John Makepeace

Wave | 2006

Kevin J. Waddell

Get Some Zs | 2005

Throughout the book, you'll find examples of old-fashioned craftsmanship and quiet sophistication. Featuring strong ties to tradition, *Cantilevered Coffee Table* (page 358) by Boykin Pearce Associates, *Walnut Desk* (page 54) by Todd A. Plummer, and *Quaker House Meeting Table* (page 169) by Carter Jason Sio each possess a no-frills, plainspoken beauty.

Tables, like most household furniture items, have an interesting history from a sociological point of view. The quality of one's furniture has always indicated socioeconomic status. In this age of cheap, ready-made, mass-produced, but oh-so-cool designed furnishings, perhaps there's no greater luxury than having a table custom built for your living space. To have the wherewithal and will to spend your time and resources acquiring a handmade table says something about you. Is the table you sought out sleek and modern? Is it elaborately carved and highly worked, reflecting untold hours of hand labor? Is it made with a rare, expensive material? Is it made from ecologically sound, sustainable materials? Is your table used often? Never? Furniture functions as a narrative of our lives in profound and surprising ways.

What brings all these tables together into this collection—and I suspect what brings you to this book—is the overarching desire to see great modern furniture craftsmanship giving shape to the classic form of the table. This book is a testament to the fact that studio furniture making is a craft that is thriving throughout the world, buoyed by a wide variety of dedicated makers and new fans, owners, and audiences.

Ray Hemachandra, *Senior Editor*

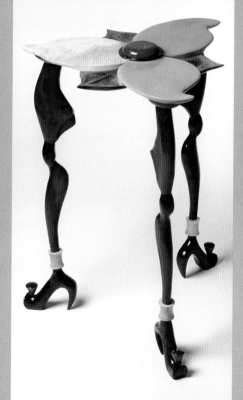

THE TABLES

Stephen Whittlesey

Mandolin | 2007

18 X 80 X 24 INCHES (45.7 X 203.2 X 61 CM)

Salvaged oak, padauk, cherry

PHOTOS BY ARTIST

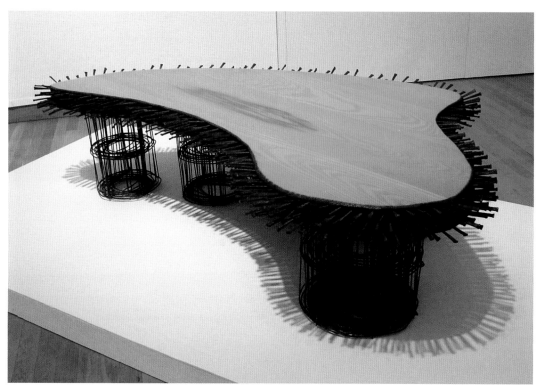

Steven T. Samson

African Nail Fetish Coffee Table | 2004

54 X 36 INCHES (137.2 X 91.4 CM)
Birch, oil paint, nails, steel mesh

PHOTOS BY JEFFREY L. MEEUWSEN

Derek Secor Davis

In the Realm of the Senses | 2004

35 X 19 X 48 INCHES (88.9 X 48.3 X 121.9 CM)

Pigmented epoxy, aspen twigs, poplar, acrylic, milk paint

PHOTO BY JOHN BONATH

Brent Harrison Skidmore

Low-Slung Boulders Table | 2005

17 X 53 X 24 INCHES (43.2 X 134.6 X 61 CM)

Ash, basswood, acrylic paint, glass

PHOTO BY DARLENE KACZMARCZYK

Wells Mason

Big White Little Red | 2008

TALLEST, 22 X 14 X 14 INCHES (55.9 X 35.6 X 35.6 CM)

Medium-density fiberboard, lacquer

PHOTO BY JIM TOBAC

Anne Bossert

Atomic Egg Side Table | 2005

23³/₄ X 32 X 22 INCHES (60.3 X 81.3 X 55.9 CM)

Baltic beech plywood, dyed hand-woven cotton cloth, glass

PHOTOS BY JOE MENDOZA

Michael C. Fortune

Fan Coffee Table | 2002

15 X 78 X 30 INCHES (38.1 X 198.1 X 76.2 CM)

Bee's wing mahogany, Macassar ebony, curly maple

PHOTO BY ARTIST

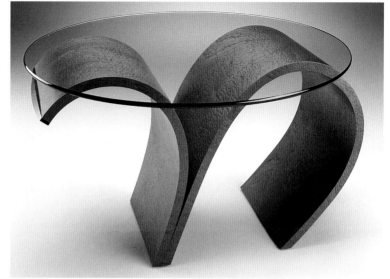

Richard Judd

Bird Table | 2002

22 X 36 X 30 INCHES (55.9 X 91.4 X 76.2 CM)
Pomele sapele veneer, bending plywood,
wenge, glass
PHOTO BY BILL LEMKE

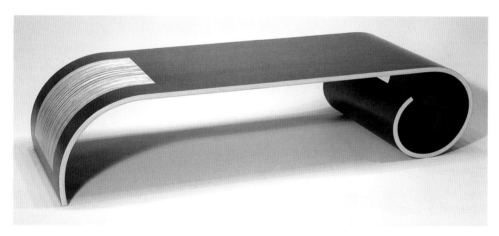

Kino Guérin

Toboggan Table | 2005

13 X 52 X 20 INCHES (33 X 132.1 X 50.8 CM)
Wenge and zebrawood veneer, laminated plywood
PHOTO BY ELYSE BÉLANGER

Dale J. Wedig

Red Line | 2004

22 X 36 X 48 INCHES (55.9 X 91.4 X 121.9 CM)

Aluminum, rubber

PHOTOS BY ARTIST

John Eric Byers

Two Squares Table | 2006

15 X 38 X 38 INCHES (38.1 X 96.5 X 96.5 CM)
Mahogany, milk paint, lacquer

PHOTOS BY ANDY GILLIS

Masafumi Sawada

Moonlight Table | 2006

$25^{9}/_{16}$ X $90^{3}/_{8}$ X $35^{7}/_{16}$ INCHES (65 X 230 X 90 CM)

Soft iron, copper, zelkova, Chinese quince

PHOTO BY TETUZO AKASAKA

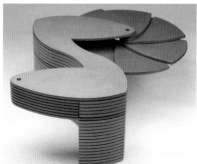

Jeremy J. Cox

Cantilever | 2006

19 1/2 X 74 X 28 INCHES (49.5 X 188 X 71.1 CM)

Synthetic hardboard, medium-density fiberboard, aluminum rod, milk paint

PHOTOS BY ARTIST

Chris Martin

In Balance | 2003

21 X 29 X 22 INCHES (53.3 X 73.7 X 55.9 CM)

Reclaimed redwood, concrete, steel, brass plumb bob

PHOTO BY GEORGE ENSLEY

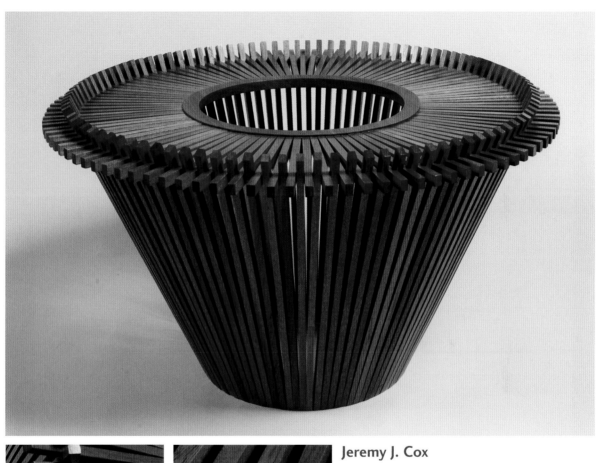

Jeremy J. Cox
Radiant | 2007

19 X 33 X 33 INCHES (48.3 X 83.8 X 83.8 CM)
Mahogany, stainless steel rod
PHOTOS BY ARTIST

John Wiggers

Solomon's Table/Desk | 2005

29 X 19 X 51 INCHES (73.7 X 48.3 X 129.5 CM)

Amboyna, birch ply, walnut, sassafras, hawthorn

PHOTO BY LORNE CHAPMAN

Eric Weil

Cone Table | 2004

16 X 36 INCHES (40.6 X 91.4 CM)

Medium-density fiberboard, colored cast concrete

PHOTO BY RYAN BENYI

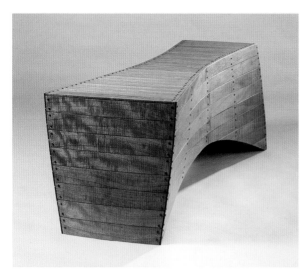

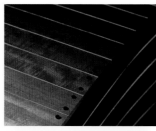

Heath Matysek-Snyder

Mahogany Twist | 2006

16 X 48 X 16 INCHES (40.6 X 121.9 X 40.6 CM)

Mahogany, nails, glow-in-the-dark paint, birch plywood

PHOTOS BY LARRY STANLEY

Jari-Pekka Vilkman

Monolith | 2006

17¹¹/₁₆ X 47¹/₄ X 47¹/₄ INCHES (45 X 120 X 120 CM)

Macassar ebony, ebony, wenge

PHOTO BY ARTIST

Andrew Clinch

Fold 3 | 2007

18 X 18 X 45 INCHES (45.7 X 45.7 X 114.3 CM)

Zebrawood

PHOTO BY JUAN HERNANDEZ

Michael Gloor

Dancer Table #2 | 2006

33 X 33 X 18 INCHES (83.8 X 83.8 X 45.7 CM)

Fiddleback anigre veneer, bloodwood, ebony, paint

PHOTO BY DAVID GILSTEIN

Taeyoul Ryu

Pive | 2007

29 X 70 X 70 INCHES (73.7 X 177.8 X 177.8 CM)

Walnut, medium-density fiberboard, silver

PHOTOS BY JOOYEON HA

Kino Guérin

Estrella Table | 2005

13 X 36 X 36 INCHES (33 X 91.4 X 91.4 CM)

Bloodwood and amazaque veneer, laminated plywood

PHOTO BY ELYSE BÉLANGER

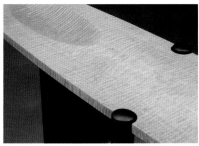

Michael C. Fortune

Entranceway Table | 2005

32 X 60 X 11 INCHES (81.3 X 152.4 X 27.9 CM)
Curly maple, Macassar ebony
PHOTOS BY ARTIST

Michael Cullen

Neptune | 2008

38 X 38 X 12 INCHES (96.5 X 96.5 X 30.5 CM)

Gabon ebony, Ceylon satinwood

PHOTO BY DON RUSSEL

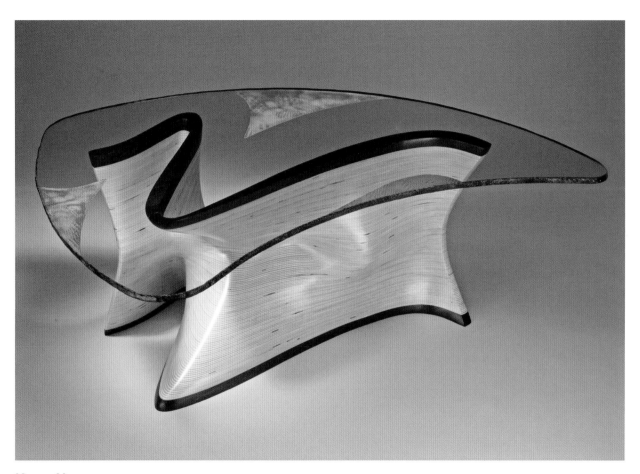

Kerry Vesper
Alisha Volotzky

Wave | 2006

19 X 45 X 32 INCHES (48.3 X 114.3 X 81.3 CM)
Baltic birch, wenge, carved and painted glass
PHOTO BY GEORGE POST

Dale Lewis

Artifishial | 2006

38 X 59 X 13½ INCHES (96.5 X 149.9 X 34.3 CM)

Curly maple, cherry, ebony, walnut, lacquer finish

PHOTO BY RALPH ANDERSON

David Hurwitz

Sugar Maple Taffy Table | 2005

27 X 6³/₈ X 12 INCHES (68.6 X 16.2 X 30.5 CM)
Vermont sugar maple, bird's-eye Vermont sugar maple
PHOTO BY ARTIST

Kerry O. Furlani
David Hurwitz

Nautilus End Table | 2006

24 X 27 X 20 INCHES (61 X 68.6 X 50.8 CM)
Vermont green slate, Vermont sugar maple, steel plate
PHOTO BY ARTIST

Aaron Levine

Eutectic | 2005

20½ X 27½ X 16 INCHES (52.1 X 69.9 X 40.6 CM)

Holly, spalted holly

PHOTO BY ART GRICE

Nicholas Chandler
Red and Curly Low Table | 2006

15³/₄ X 27⁹/₁₆ X 13³/₄ INCHES (40 X 70 X 35 CM)
Birch, red lacquer
PHOTO BY INDUFOTO

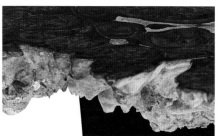

Laura Bergsøe

Table for Goldsmith Shop | 2007

36 5/8 X 51 3/16 X 39 3/4 INCHES (93 X 130 X 101 CM)

Elm burr, leather, steel, medium-density fiberboard, Oregon pine

PHOTOS BY MARC FLURI

Scott Grove

Polyidol | 2005

33 X 36 X 10 INCHES (83.8 X 91.4 X 25.4 CM)

Sycamore, big walnut, palm, amber, silver, mother-of-pearl, amethyst, turquoise, onyx, malachite

PHOTO BY JOHN SMILLIE

Michael A. Gregorio

Portals | 2005

26 X 34 X 19 INCHES (66 X 86.4 X 48.3 CM)

Bleached bigleaf maple burl, tiger maple, stain, lacquer

PHOTO BY ARTIST

Bart Niswonger
Carl Schlerman

Peanut Table | 2005

18 X 33 X 19 INCHES (45.7 X 83.8 X 48.3 CM)

Ash, ebonized ash, dye, catalyzed urethane

PHOTO BY ARTIST

Bart Niswonger

Bedside Tables | 2007

21 X 21 X 21 INCHES (53.3 X 53.3 X 53.3 CM)
Ash, dye, catalyzed urethane, cast urethane
PHOTOS BY ARTIST

Myung Rye Kim
Invitation | 1999

16$^1/_2$ X 30$^5/_{16}$ X 8$^1/_4$ INCHES (42 X 77 X 21 CM)
Ceramic, underglaze, black glaze
PHOTO BY ARTIST

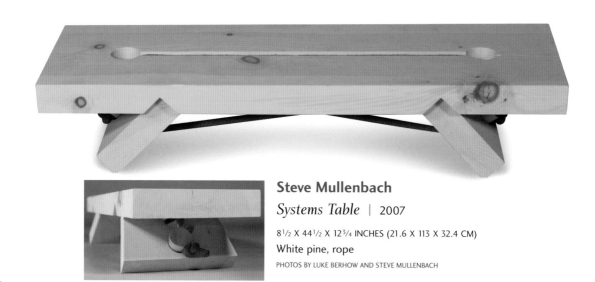

Steve Mullenbach
Systems Table | 2007

8$^1/_2$ X 44$^1/_2$ X 12$^3/_4$ INCHES (21.6 X 113 X 32.4 CM)
White pine, rope
PHOTOS BY LUKE BERHOW AND STEVE MULLENBACH

Timothy Maddox

Change the Focus | 2007

15 X 37 X 23 INCHES (38.1 X 94 X 58.4 CM)

Steel, sycamore, patina, ink, charcoal

PHOTOS BY TIM BARNWELL

Michael Singer

Entry Table | 2004

34 X 48 X 9 INCHES (86.4 X 121.9 X 22.9 CM)

Quilted Western maple, sycamore, ebony, aluminum

PHOTO BY PAUL SCHRAUB

Kerry O. Furlani
David Hurwitz

Tree of Life Hall Table | 2007

36 X 48 X 11 INCHES (91.4 X 121.9 X 27.9 CM)
Vermont green slate, cherry

PHOTOS BY ARTISTS

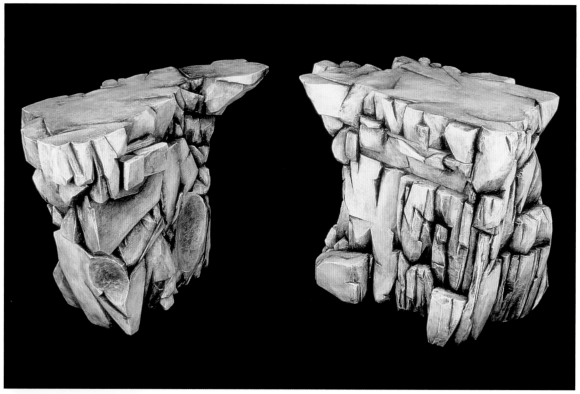

Travis Townsend

Bedside End Tables: Hers and His | 1998

EACH, 23 X 23 X 17 INCHES (58.4 X 58.4 X 43.2 CM)

Carved basswood, acrylic paint

PHOTOS BY ARTIST

David Greenwood

Slice of Life (for CES) | 2006

90 X 96 X 60 INCHES (228.6 X 243.8 X 152.4 CM)

Pine, steel, stain

PHOTOS BY ARTIST

Robert A. Griffith

Console Table | 2003

35 X 28 X 14 INCHES (88.9 X 71.1 X 35.6 CM)

Tubular steel, ash

PHOTO BY LISA HINKLE

Jan Wehrens

Table | 1999

16¹/₂ X 20⁷/₁₆ X 20⁷/₁₆ INCHES (42 X 52 X 52 CM)

Steel, paint, glass

PHOTO BY ANGELA BRÖHAN

Srdjan Simić

Nivoi | 2005

18 X 36 X 36 INCHES (45.7 X 91.4 X 91.4 CM)

Powder-coated square tubular steel, glass panels

PHOTO BY ARTIST

Douglas E. Fanning

Cross 2 | 2006

72 X 46 X 30 INCHES (182.9 X 116.8 X 76.2 CM)

Wood

PHOTO BY NATHAN SAYERS

Bob Marsh

Barb | 2006

20 X 18 X 19 INCHES (50.8 X 45.7 X 48.3 CM)

Poplar, cast resin, paint

PHOTO BY ARTIST

Chulyeon Park

D Table | 2008

20 X 10 X 61 INCHES (50.8 X 25.4 X 154.9 CM)
Steel, powder coating, walnut

PHOTOS BY LARRY STANLEY

ducduc

The Table | 2005

30 X 91 ½ X 41 ½ INCHES
(76.2 X 232.4 X 105.4 CM)

Walnut, poplar

PHOTOS BY ARTIST

Todd A. Plummer

Walnut Desk | 2007

29 X 19 X 48 INCHES (73.7 X 48.3 X 121.9 CM)

Walnut, maple, fir, beech, manzanita

PHOTO BY ARTIST

Jerry Rosenberger

Inspiration of Emperor Fu His | 2008

26 X 15 X 15 INCHES (66 X 38.1 X 38.1 CM)
Kabukali, padauk, maple, ebony, tatabu
PHOTO BY ARTIST

Jerry Rosenberger

Chess on Rosewood | 2006

24³/₄ X 17¹/₂ X 17¹/₂ INCHES (62.9 X 44.5 X 44.5 CM)
Bolivian rosewood, cocobolo, French olivewood
PHOTO BY ARTIST

Matthew Michael Gilliland
Untitled | 2006

19 X 30 X 30 INCHES (48.3 X 76.2 X 76.2 CM)
Hard maple, walnut, cherry, polyurethane finish
PHOTO BY DON LIUTNER

Harold R. Pollard

Sofa Table | 2005

36 X 60 X 17 INCHES (91.4 X 152.4 X 43.2 CM)

Michigan swamp white oak, wenge, red oak

PHOTO BY DOUGLAS URNER

Kerry Vesper

Altar Table | 2004

36 X 60 X 26 INCHES (91.4 X 152.4 X 66 CM)
Sapele, Baltic birch, wenge

PHOTO BY RANDALL BOHL

John McDermott

Corner Table | 1988

35 X 35 X 21 INCHES (88.9 X 88.9 X 53.3 CM)

Black cherry

PHOTOS BY TIM BARNWELL

David Colwell

TS Table | 1999

28⁵/₁₆ X 51³/₁₆ X 51³/₁₆ INCHES
(72 X 130 X 130 CM)

Ash, polished toughened glass,
steel spider, steel cable, rubber
suction cups

PHOTO BY ARTIST

Richard Bronk

Untitled | 2004

18 X 36 X 36 INCHES (45.7 X 91.4 X 91.4 CM)

Cherry, various maples, spalted maple, wenge, glass top

PHOTO BY WILLIAM LEMKE

Po Shun Leong

City | 2000

16 X 60 INCHES (40.6 X 152.4 CM)

Mahogany, buckeye burl, cherry burl, bleached maple,
pink ivory wood, pau amarelo, narra, palm, ebony,
bocote, koa, purpleheart, gold leaf

PHOTOS BY ARTIST

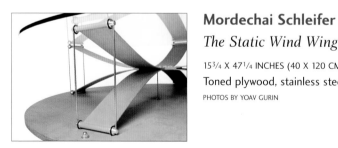

Mordechai Schleifer

The Static Wind Wing | 2003

15³/₄ X 47¹/₄ INCHES (40 X 120 CM)
Toned plywood, stainless steel, glass

PHOTOS BY YOAV GURIN

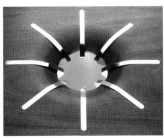

Richard Prisco

Synchronized Swimming | 2007

15 X 52 INCHES (38.1 X 132.1 CM)
Mahogany, polished aluminum

PHOTOS BY JOSEPH BYRD

Jeff Soderbergh
Anne Black Side Table | 2002

33 X 48 X 19 INCHES (83.8 X 121.9 X 48.3 CM)
Reclaimed poplar blacksmith sign cornice
(circa 1700), Vermont maple
PHOTO BY BILL DURVIN

Michael J. Gilmartin
Empire Console Table | 1996

32 X 64 X 16 INCHES (81.3 X 162.6 X 40.6 CM)
Marine fir plywood, wenge
PHOTO BY CHARLEY AKERS

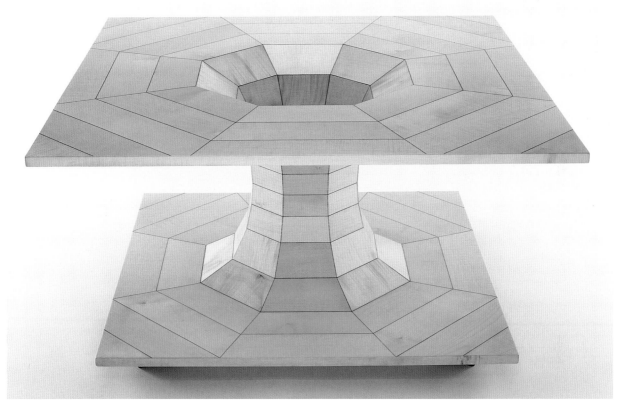

Fred Baier

Black Hole Table | 2004

39³/₈ X 39³/₈ X 39³/₈ INCHES (1 X 1 X 1 METER)

English sycamore

PHOTO BY DUNCAN SMITH

Irve W. Dell

Tool for Dining | 1993

29 X 40 X 74 INCHES (73.7 X 101.6 X 188 CM)

Steel, mahogany, bronze, glass

PHOTO BY STEVE SCHNEIDER

Fred Baier

Tool to Place Things in the Here and Now | 2004

17 $^{11}/_{16}$ X 13 $^{3}/_{4}$ INCHES (45 X 35 CM)

Stained sycamore, anodized aluminum

PHOTO BY BOO BEAUMENT

Eric Weil

Parallel Roller | 2006

17 X 22 X 40 INCHES (43.2 X 55.9 X 101.6 CM)

Colored concrete, walnut, locking casters

PHOTO BY RYAN BENYI

Jari-Pekka Vilkman

Coastline Sofa Table | 2006

17 11/16 X 51 3/16 X 21 5/8 INCHES (45 X 130 X 55 CM)
Teak
PHOTO BY ARTIST

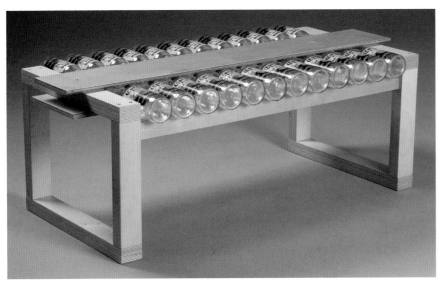

Adrian B. French

Corona Table | 2004

14 X 40 X 22 INCHES (35.6 X 101.6 X 55.9 CM)
Birch plywood, beer bottles
PHOTO BY LARRY STANLEY

Laura Rittenhouse

Untitled | 2003

31 X 36 X 72 INCHES (78.7 X 91.4 X 182.9 CM)

Teak

PHOTOS BY BERRY GOYETTE

Joe Lastomirsky

End Table with Vase | 2002

20 X 18 X 15 INCHES (50.8 X 45.7 X 38.1 CM)

Concrete, bamboo

PHOTO BY MARK HOOPER

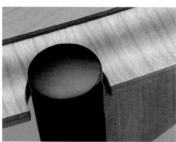

Michael C. Fortune

Side Table | 2007

30 X 76 X 12 INCHES (76.2 X 193 X 30.5 CM)

Cherry, Macassar ebony

PHOTOS BY ARTIST

William Thomas

Sheraton Breakfast Table | 2005

28 X 32 X 44 INCHES (71.1 X 81.3 X 111.8 CM)

Mahogany, crotch mahogany, satinwood veneers

PHOTOS BY BILL TRUSLOW

David Upfill-Brown

Stuck's Table | 2007

29 X 60 X 120 INCHES (73.7 X 152.4 X 304.8 CM)

Poplar, cherry, cherry veneer, milk paint

PHOTOS BY JIM DUGAN

Mark Sfirri

Walking Table | 1995

24 X 16 X 24 INCHES (61 X 40.6 X 61 CM)

Curly maple, mahogany

PHOTO BY ARTIST

William D. Bolstad

Prickly-Edged Table | 2006

25 X 29 X 30 INCHES (63.5 X 73.7 X 76.2 CM)

Spalted maple burl, ebonized walnut

PHOTO BY DAN KUITKA

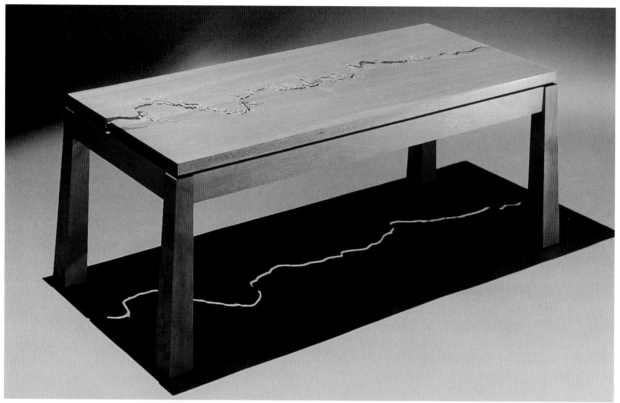

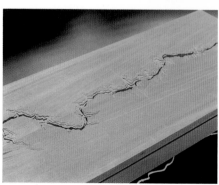

Phillip Mann

Lodore Canyon Table | 2000

16 X 18 X 48 INCHES (40.6 X 45.7 X 121.9 CM)

Honduran mahogany

PHOTOS BY JIM KREBS

Steve Holman

Temple Table | 1998

18 X 48 X 22 INCHES (45.7 X 121.9 X 55.9 CM)

Cherry, figured maple, wenge

PHOTO BY COOK NEILSON

Kevin-Louis Barton

Contradiction Coffee Table | 2001

20 X 48 X 26 INCHES (50.8 X 121.9 X 66 CM)
Walnut, glass
PHOTO BY ARTIST

Ric Allison

Slacken Pair | 1999

18 X 17 X 21 INCHES (45.7 X 43.2 X 53.3 CM)

Macassar ebony, Gabon ebony, machiche

PHOTO BY ARTIST

R. Thomas Tedrowe, Jr.

Soleil Table | 1998

30 X 42 INCHES (76.2 X 106.7 CM)

Macassar ebony, Honduran mahogany

PHOTO BY ARTIST

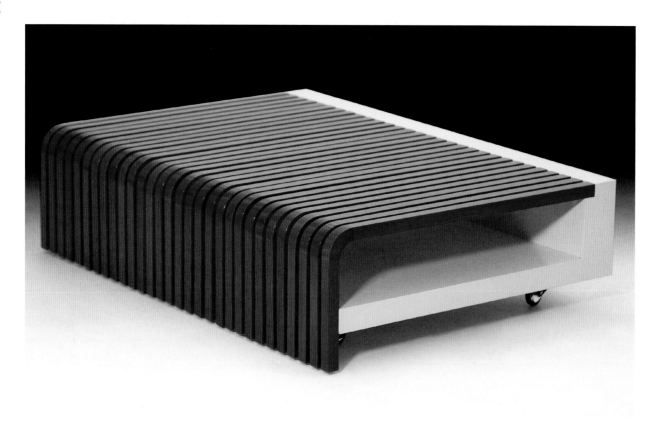

David Potts

Rail Table | 2005

12³/₁₆ X 47¹/₄ X 32¹/₂ INCHES (31 X 120 X 82.5 CM)

African mahogany, medium-density fiberboard, clear gloss, powder coat

PHOTO BY MICK BRADLEY

Monika Olejnik

Reformed Coffee Table | 2007

15 X 18 X 48 INCHES (38.1 X 45.7 X 121.9 CM)

Sassafras, India ink, powder-coated steel

PHOTO BY ARTIST

John Quan

San Coffee Table | 2006

8 1/2 X 35 7/16 X 23 5/8 INCHES (21.5 X 90 X 60 CM)

American walnut veneer, medium-density fiberboard, plywood, furniture wax

PHOTO BY GRANT HANCOCK

Stephen Hogbin

Connection | 2005

27 X 34 X 19 INCHES (68.6 X 86.4 X 48.3 CM)

Ash, paint, glass

PHOTO BY ARTIST

Ryan P. Seiler

Pierced Coffee Table | 2008

16³/₄ X 47 X 18 INCHES (42.5 X 119.4 X 45.7 CM)

Mahogany, milk paint, linseed oil

PHOTO BY GEORGE ENSLEY

Stephen Hogbin

Clarity | 2006

35 X 18 INCHES (88.9 X 45.7 CM)

Ebonized wood, maple, glass

PHOTO BY ARTIST

Lepo

Untitled | 2006

38 X 28 X 48 INCHES (96.5 X 71.1 X 121.9 CM)

Cherry, maple, cocobolo, acrylic

PHOTO BY MICHAEL J. AYERS

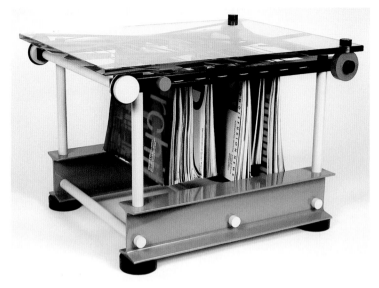

Gabriel Luis Romeu
Magazine End Table | 2005

17 X 24 X 20 INCHES (43.2 X 61 X 50.8 CM)
Aluminum, stainless steel cable, O rings,
powder coat, glass
PHOTO BY ARTIST

Peter Loh
Satellite | 2004

19 X 22 X 15 INCHES (48.3 X 55.9 X 38.1 CM)
Pearwood, Bolivian rosewood, birch
plywood, aluminum, rubber
PHOTO BY ARTIST

John Makepeace

Wave | 2006

65 X 32 INCHES (165 X 82 CM)
Oak, aluminum
PHOTO BY ARTIST

Seth Rolland

Tsubo Coffee Table | 2007

17 X 55 X 27 INCHES (43.2 X 139.7 X 68.6 CM)

Salvaged mahogany, granite

PHOTO BY FRANK ROSS

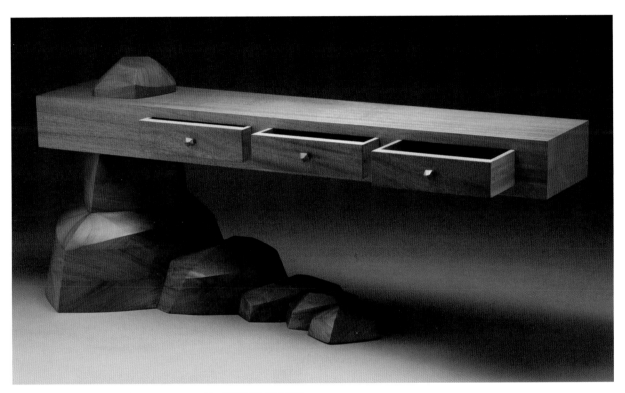

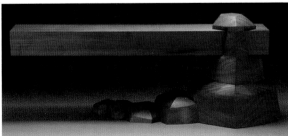

James P. McNabb

Three-Drawer Table | 2007

53 X 23 X 21 INCHES (134.6 X 58.4 X 53.3 CM)

Mahogany, steel

PHOTOS BY ETC PHOTOGRAPHY

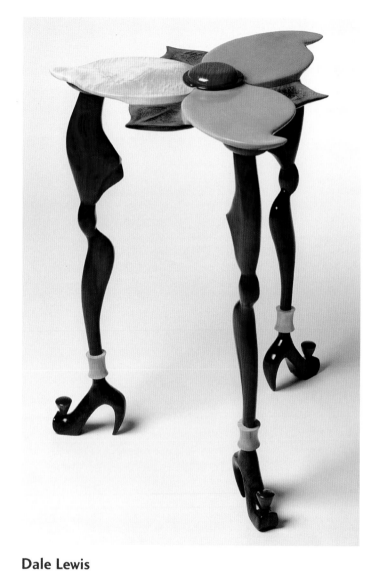

Dale Lewis

Ruby Begonia | 2004

36 X 26 X 25 INCHES (91.4 X 66 X 63.5 CM)

Curly maple, cherry, lacquer finish

PHOTO BY RALPH ANDERSON

Ken Richards
Demilune Hall Table | 2002

31 X 42 X 14 INCHES (78.7 X 106.7 X 35.6 CM)
Figured imbuya, figured maple
PHOTO BY ROBERT L. MCCRORY

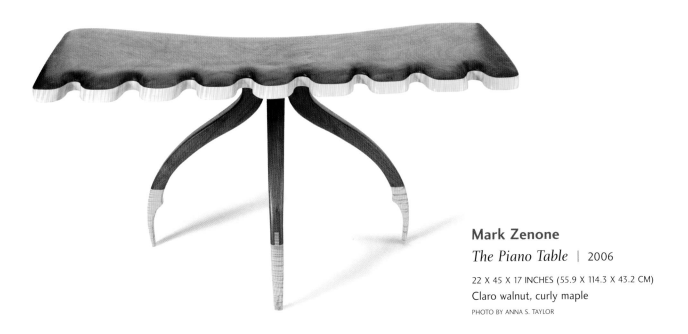

Mark Zenone
The Piano Table | 2006

22 X 45 X 17 INCHES (55.9 X 114.3 X 43.2 CM)
Claro walnut, curly maple
PHOTO BY ANNA S. TAYLOR

Michael Cullen

The Lilies | 2006

31 X 10¹/₂ X 27 INCHES (78.7 X 26.7 X 68.6 CM)

Bubinga

PHOTO BY DON RUSSEL

Karen Ernst

Bilateral Table | 2006

29 X 48 X 60 INCHES (73.7 X 121.9 X 152.4 CM)

Walnut, curly maple, milk paint

PHOTO BY ARTIST

William Laberge

*Custom Mahogany
Dining Table* | 2002

60 X 20 X 30 INCHES
(152.4 X 50.8 X 76.2 CM)

African ribbon-stripe mahogany,
ebony inlay, brass casters

PHOTOS BY JOHN A. CONTE

Josh Metcalf

Henry II Walnut Dining Table | 2005

29 X 94 X 34 INCHES (73.7 X 238.8 X 86.4 CM)

Walnut, walnut burl, boxwood, ivory, ebony, satinwood

PHOTO BY ARTIST

James Schriber

Leaf Table | 2006

29 X 44 X 92 INCHES (73.7 X 111.8 X 233.7 CM)

Cherry

PHOTOS BY JOHN KANE

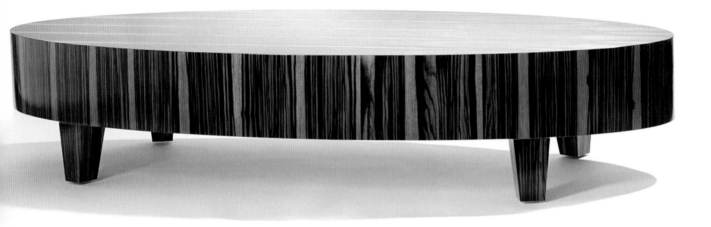

Anton Gerner

Oval Coffee Table | 2008

17 11/16 X 66 13/16 X 31 1/2 INCHES (45 X 170 X 80 CM)

Macassar ebony veneer

PHOTO BY ARTIST

Floyd Gompf

Homage to FLW: Coffee Table | 2005

20 X 35 X 18 INCHES (50.8 X 88.9 X 45.7 CM)

Found wood

PHOTO BY RICHARD HELLYER

John Wiggers

Whale Tail Table/Desk | 2002

32 X 75½ X 57½ INCHES
(81.3 X 191.8 X 146.1 CM)

Macassar ebony, birch ply, anthracite

PHOTOS BY JOHN GLOS

John M. Godfrey

Untitled | 2007

33 X 43 X 19 INCHES (83.8 X 109.2 X 48.3 CM)

Ebonized ash, cherry

PHOTO BY JIM DUGAN

Jacque Allen

My Drawing Board | 2006

36 X 42 X 28 INCHES (91.4 X 106.7 X 71.1 CM)

Mahogany, maple, chalkboard, aluminum

PHOTO BY ARTIST

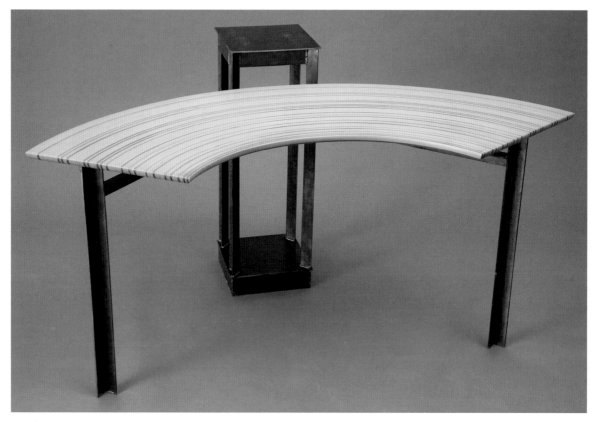

Stefan Furrer

Surfboard | 1999

30 X 55 X 34 INCHES (76.2 X 139.7 X 86.4 CM)

Maple, walnut, angle iron

PHOTO BY JOHN BIRCHARD

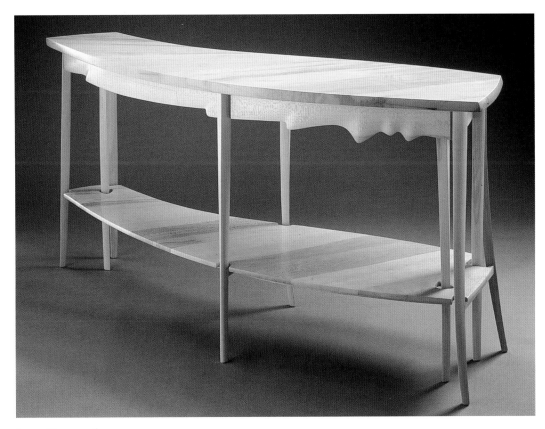

Jere Osgood

Wave Table | 1999

28 X 62 X 20 INCHES (71.1 X 157.5 X 50.8 CM)

Sycamore

PHOTO BY DEAN POWELL

Neil Erasmus

Sept Hall Table | 2008

90 X 120 X 42 INCHES (228.6 X 304.8 X 106.7 CM)
Blackbutt veneers, medium-density fiberboard
torsion box, leather, acrylic

PHOTOS BY ROBERT GARVEY

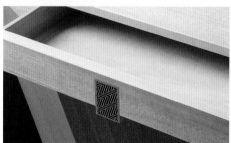

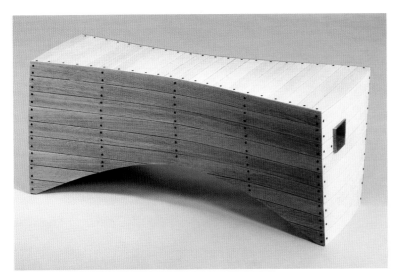

Heath Matysek-Snyder
Oak Twist | 2006

16 X 36 X 16 INCHES (40.6 X 91.4 X 40.6 CM)

Bleached and natural white oak, nails, birch plywood

PHOTOS BY LARRY STANLEY

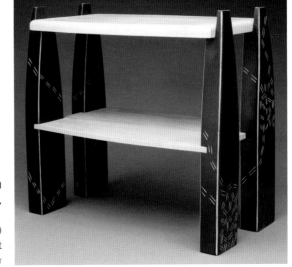

Jacque Allen
Tracks in the Snow | 2007

20 X 22 X 12 INCHES (50.8 X 55.9 X 30.5 CM)

Maple, basswood, paint

PHOTO BY ARTIST

Todd Ouwehand

Lo Coffee Table | 2001

14 X 60 X 40 INCHES (35.6 X 152.4 X 101.6 CM)

Maple, quilted maple, wenge

PHOTO BY ALAN TOMLINSON

Ken Edwards

Chubbler #6 | 2000

21 X 26 X 26 INCHES (53.3 X 66 X 66 CM)
Medium-density fiberboard, acrylic
PHOTO BY KIM HARRINGTON

John Eric Byers

Open Form Tables 1 & 2 | 2007

20 X 14 X 14 INCHES (50.8 X 35.6 X 35.6 CM)

Mahogany, milk paint, lacquer

PHOTO BY ANDY GILLIS

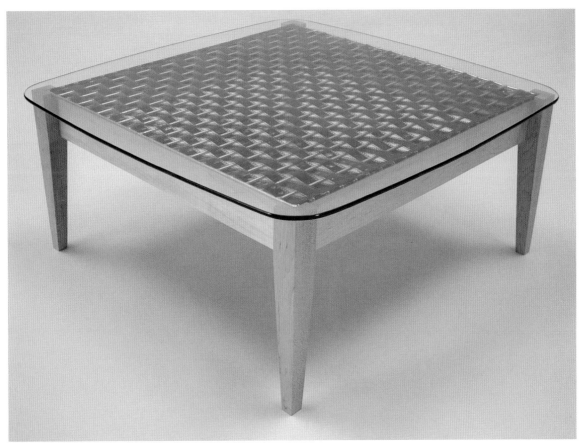

Christy Oates

Film Table | 2003

14 X 36 X 36 INCHES (35.6 X 91.4 X 91.4 CM)

Film, maple, steel, glass

PHOTOS BY ARTIST

Todd A. Plummer

Tambour Coffee Table | 2005

17 X 19 X 43 INCHES (43.2 X 48.3 X 109.2 CM)

Poplar, maple, myrtle

PHOTO BY ARTIST

Asher N. Dunn

Princess Anne Bedside Table | 2007

18 X 16 X 14 1/2 INCHES (45.7 X 40.6 X 36.8 CM)
Plywood
PHOTOS BY ARTIST

Oliver Drake

End Tables | 2007

22 7/16 X 15 5/16 X 15 5/16 INCHES (57 X 39 X 39 CM)
Maple, walnut, yew, limestone from the
island of Symi, Greece
PHOTO BY PAUL BOX

Rush Skinnell

Separate but One Coffee Table | 2004

16 1/2 X 55 X 24 1/2 INCHES (41.9 X 139.7 X 62.2 CM)

Ash

PHOTO BY JOHN LUCAS

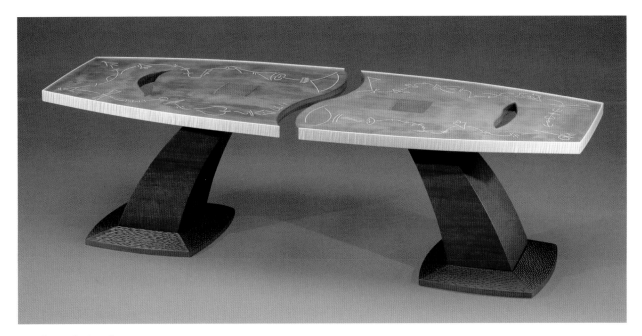

Mark Del Guidice

Split Coffee Table | 2003

18 X 60 X 24 INCHES (45.7 X 152.4 X 61 CM)

Mahogany, curly maple, medium-density fiberboard, milk paint

PHOTO BY CLEMENTS/HOWCROFT

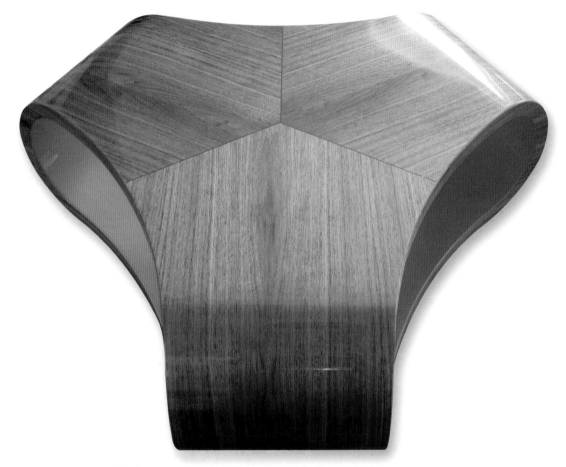

Melia
(Partners: John-Paul Melia and Lucy Tatam)
Large Pants Coffee Table | *2006*

11 13/16 X 357/16 X 279/16 INCHES (30 X 90 X 70 CM)

Walnut veneer, orange paint lacquer, medium-density fiberboard

PHOTO BY LUCY TATAM

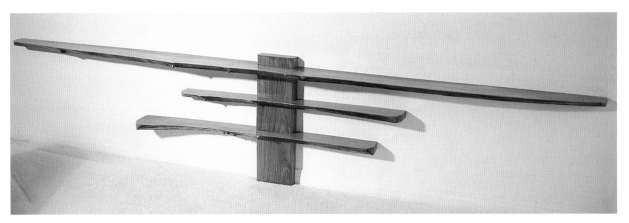

Dave Hergesheimer
Wall Table | 2005

108 X 24 X 7¹/₂ INCHES (274.3 X 60.9 X 19 CM)
Western and American black walnut
PHOTO BY ARTIST

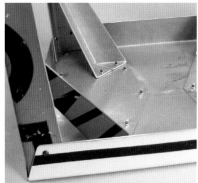

Boris Bally
Small Square Transit Table | 2006

18 X 18 X 20 INCHES (45.7 X 45.7 X 101.6 CM)
Recycled aluminum traffic signs, recycled
aluminum tube, steel hardware, champagne corks
PHOTOS BY ARTIST

Marcus C. Papay

Linear Discontinuity | 2007

19 X 60 INCHES (48.3 X 152.4 CM)

Hard maple, steel

PHOTOS BY LARRY STANLEY

Michael Puryear

Desk | 1999

29 X 60 X 48 INCHES (73.7 X 152.4 X 121.9 CM)

Ash, wenge

PHOTO BY ARTIST

Miles Epstein

Coastal Table | 2002

14 X 48 X 56 INCHES (35.6 X 121.9 X 142.2 CM)

Salvaged lumber, steel

PHOTO BY ARTIST

Jeff Wallin

Tsunami Table | 2006

17 X 48 X 16 INCHES (43.2 X 121.9 X 40.6 CM)

Mild steel, rust patina

PHOTO BY KEITH COTTON

Jeremy J. Cox

Cadence | 2007

21 X 34¹/₂ X 30¹/₂ INCHES (53.3 X 87.6 X 77.5 CM)

Redwood, wenge

PHOTO BY MATTHIAS PLIESSNIG

Sunhee Oh

Crowd of Emotion | 2005

16 X 30 X 18 INCHES (40.6 X 76.2 X 45.7 CM)
Walnut

PHOTO BY ELIZABETH LAMARK

Marianne Lattanzio Albanese

Writer's Table | 2006

32 X 60 X 34 INCHES (81.3 X 152.4 X 86.4 CM)

Cherry, ambrosia maple, sugar maple,
pink ivory, azure stone

PHOTO BY GENE SMIRNOV

Jeremy J. Cox

Formation | 2007

23 X 18 X 22 INCHES (58.4 X 45.7 X 55.9 CM)

Butternut, white oak, cotton strip

PHOTOS BY MATTHIAS PLIESSNIG

Taeyoul Ryu

Poseidon | 2006

29 X 55 X 14 INCHES (73.7 X 139.7 X 35.6 CM)

White oak, medium-density fiberboard

PHOTOS BY JOOYEON HA

Dean Vande Griend

Digital Table | 2005

16 X 48 X 24 INCHES (40.6 X 121.9 X 61 CM)

Maple

PHOTO BY GEORGE ENSLEY

Mark Alan Koons

Sky King Table | 1999

32 X 36 X 24 INCHES (81.3 X 91.4 X 61 CM)

Walnut, butternut, sassafras, maple, red gum, ash, box elder, cherry, willow, lilac, epoxy finish

PHOTO BY ARTIST

Craig Nutt

Green Asparagus Table with Drawers | 1992

30 X 42 X 19 INCHES (76.2 X 106.7 X 48.3 CM)
Purpleheart, pau amarelo, oil paint
PHOTO BY RICKEY YANAURA

Mark Del Guidice

Table for All Reasons | 2007

30 X 33 X 33 INCHES (76.2 X 83.8 X 83.8 CM)
Bubinga, basswood, milk paint
PHOTO BY CLEMENTS/HOWCROFT

David Haig

Sally's Hall Table | 2008

35 X 59 X 12 INCHES (90 X 150 X 30 CM)

Matai, silver beech, ebony

PHOTO BY DANIEL ALLEN

Seth Rolland

Parabola Side Table | 2006

22 X 40 X 21 INCHES (55.9 X 101.6 X 53.3 CM)

Walnut, ash, glass

PHOTOS BY FRANK ROSS

John Clark

Serving Table | 2000

36 X 20 X 64 INCHES (91.4 X 50.8 X 162.6 CM)

Mahogany, ebony, granite

PHOTO BY ARTIST

Keaton Freeman

Drafting Table | 2006

37 X 36 X 24 INCHES (94 X 91.4 X 61 CM)
Cherry
PHOTO BY ARTIST

Todd Ouwehand

Arched Side Table | 2007

19 X 16 X 16 INCHES (48.3 X 40.6 X 40.6 CM)
Walnut, zebrawood
PHOTO BY ALAN TOMLINSON

Mark S. Levin

Locatelli Leaf Side Table | 2006

22 X 43 X 22 INCHES (55.9 X 109.2 X 55.9 CM)
Cherry
PHOTOS BY MARGOT GEIST

Po Shun Leong

Centipede | 2007

LARGEST, 20 X 30 X 20 INCHES (50.8 X 76.2 X 50.8 CM)

Maple, maple dowels

PHOTO BY ARTIST

Donald H. Moss

Ice Table | 2006

31 X 35 X 23 INCHES (78.7 X 88.9 X 58.4 CM)

White birch, black grout, etched glass, wire

PHOTO BY SCOTT VAN SICKLIN

Gary A. Leake

Nature's Rhythm Hall Table | 2007

30 X 54¹/₂ X 11¹/₄ INCHES (76.2 X 138.4 X 28.6 CM)

Claro black walnut

PHOTO BY MICHAEL STADLER

Glen Guarino

Purpleheart Hall Table | 1999

35 X 68 X 15 INCHES (88.9 X 172.7 X 38.1 CM)

Purpleheart

PHOTO BY RICH RUSSO PHOTOGRAPHY

Jay Whyte

Tablecloth Table | 2005

32 X 45 X 14 INCHES (81.3 X 114.3 X 35.6 CM)
Quilted maple, walnut
PHOTO BY ARTIST

Seth Rolland

North Beach Hall Table | 2005

32 X 61 X 15 INCHES (81.3 X 154.9 X 38.1 CM)

European beech, natural stone

PHOTO BY FRANK ROSS

Burt Levy

Forms Coffee Table | 2005

17 X 42 X 84 INCHES (43.2 X 106.7 X 213.4 CM)

Figured English sycamore, cherry burl, claro walnut,
English brown oak

PHOTO BY ARTIST

Alice Porembski

Untitled | 2006

24 X 92 X 18 INCHES (61 X 233.7 X 45.7 CM)
Lacewood, California walnut, ebony details
PHOTOS BY HARVEY SPECTOR

Brian Bright

Baby Killer | 2004

17 X 18 X 72 INCHES
(43.2 X 45.7 X 182.9 CM)
Walnut
PHOTO BY ARTIST

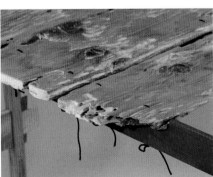

Stephen Whittlesey

Bee Board Table | 2006

35 X 41 X 16½ INCHES (88.9 X 104.1 X 40.6 CM)

Pine boards from old beehive, padauk, string

PHOTOS BY ARTIST

Bruce Schwager

Madrone Low Table | 2007

17 X 32 X 53 INCHES (43.2 X 81.3 X 134.6 CM)

Pacific madrone burl, madrona

PHOTO BY MICHAEL STADLER

Brian A. Hubel

Butterfly | 2002

30 X 108 X 40 INCHES (76.2 X 274.3 X 101.6 CM)

Mahogany, wenge

PHOTO BY DON JONES

Brad Smith

Checker Table with Spider Base | 2007

30 X 35 X 35 INCHES (76.2 X 88.9 X 88.9 CM)
Mixed hardwoods, turned oak post, found steel base

PHOTO BY JOSH GOLEMAN

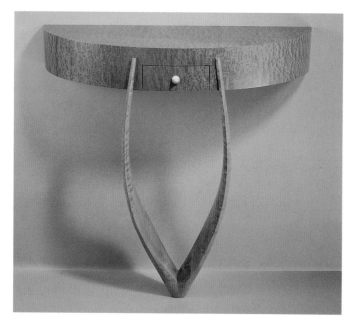

Charles B. Cobb

Wall-Hung Side Table | 1996

36 X 36 X 13 INCHES (91.4 X 91.4 X 33 CM)
Sapele veneers, quilted maple,
medium-density fiberboard

PHOTO BY HAP SAKWA

Don Green

Vespa End Tables | 2005

27 X 24 X 24 INCHES (68.6 X 61 X 61 CM)

Mahogany

PHOTOS BY ARTIST

Craig Nutt

Onion Blossom Table | 1997

29 X 16 X 16 INCHES (73.7 X 40.6 X 40.6 CM)

Cherry, oil paint

PHOTO BY JOHN LUCAS

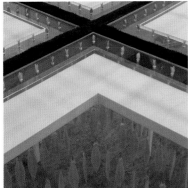

Nicole Jacquard

Greenhouse | 2004

60 X 48 X 48 INCHES (152.4 X 121.9 X 121.9 CM)
Poplar, paint, sterling silver, nylon, porcelain,
steel, grass, clear plastic sheeting
PHOTOS BY ARTIST

Michael Puryear

Arch Coffee Table | 1998

15³/₄ X 48¹/₂ X 27³/₄ INCHES (40 X 123.2 X 70.5 CM)

Ash

PHOTO BY ARTIST

Yang-Jun Kwon

Reverie and Confirmation: Contradance of East and West | 2005

26½ X 39 X 14¾ INCHES (67.3 X 99.1 X 37.5 CM)

Birch, milk paint

PHOTO BY HAYASHI KOICHIRO

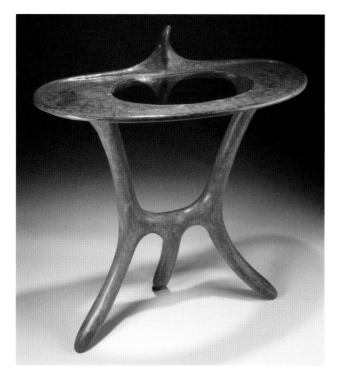

Charles A. Sthreshley

Wall Hall Table | 1992

41 X 37 X 16 INCHES (104.1 X 94 X 40.6 CM)

Concrete, glass

PHOTO BY ARTIST

Stephen Hogbin

Fragmenting S. Play | 2004

35 X 20 X 13 INCHES (88.9 X 50.8 X 33 CM)

Ash, maple, paint

PHOTO BY ARTIST

Anne Bossert

Black Tie Hall Table | 2005

30 X 48 X 12 INCHES (76.2 X 121.9 X 30.5 CM)

Baltic birch plywood, dyed hand-woven cotton cloth, glass

PHOTOS BY JOE MENDOZA

Gareth James Brown

Table of Mirrors | 2007

90¹/₈ X 28⁵/₁₆ X 28⁵/₁₆ INCHES (230 X 72 X 72 CM)

Mahogany, American walnut, burr walnut veneer, medium-density fiberboard, mirror, black lacquer

PHOTO BY GRANT HANCOCK

Michael A. Gregorio

Let Us Prey | 2007

30 X 48 INCHES (76.2 X 121.9 CM)

Walnut burl, mahogany, tiger maple, shellac, milk paint

PHOTO BY ARTIST

Bailey Humbert Heck

Jaffe Table | 2004

30 X 36 X 138 INCHES (76.2 X 91.4 X 350.5 CM)

Solid cherry, stainless steel, clear tempered float glass

PHOTOS BY ARTIST

Jacob M. Kulin

Coffee Table | 2008

16 X 36 X 36 INCHES (40.6 X 91.4 X 91.4 CM)
Glass, steel, reclaimed white oak and chestnut
PHOTO BY ARTIST

Arnt Arntzen

Heli Desk | 2000

30 X 70 X 30 INCHES (76.2 X 177.8 X 76.2 CM)

Tungsten and aluminum helicopter rotors, glass, ekki, stainless steel, lacquer

PHOTO BY GORAN BASARIC

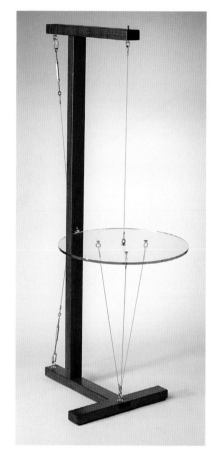

Tyson Atwell

DJ End Table | 2000

70 X 24 X 34 INCHES (177.8 X 61 X 86.4 CM)

Clear lacquered jarrah, acrylic plastic, sterling silver aircraft cable, sterling silver hardware

PHOTO BY KALLAN NISHIMOTO

Paulus Wanrooij

Oceana Demilune | 2007

33 X 40 X 20 INCHES (83.8 X 101.6 X 50.8 CM)

Walnut, maple, sapele

PHOTO BY DENNIS GRIGGS

Katherine L. Martin

Katherine's Trio | 2004

30 X 30 INCHES (76.2 X 76.2 CM)
Steel, glass
PHOTO BY BRIAN L. MOSHER

Kevin Ross Blomenkamp

Nautical Table | 2004

5 X 5 X 5 INCHES (12.7 X 12.7 X 12.7 CM)
Brass, steel, acrylic
PHOTO BY ARTIST

Christy Oates

Film Reel Table | 2006

30 X 23 X 23 INCHES (76.2 X 58.4 X 58.4 CM)

Film reel, steel, glass

PHOTO BY ARTIST

Bob Marsh

Table I | 2005

37 X 84 X 42 INCHES (94 X 213.4 X 106.7 CM)

Cast resin, cast concrete, glass, paint

PHOTOS BY ARTIST

Douglas E. Sigler

Door Coffee Table | 2003

18 X 22 X 40 INCHES (45.7 X 55.9 X 101.6 CM)
Ash, leather, doorknob
PHOTO BY ARTIST

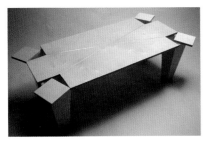

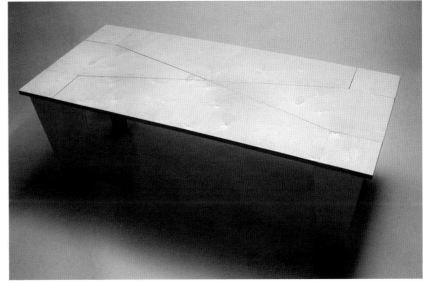

Justin Dehner

Zen | 2003

17¹/₂ X 54 X 24 INCHES (44.5 X 137.2 X 61 CM)
Baltic birch plywood, aluminum
PHOTOS BY ARTIST

Gabriel Luis Romeu

Tensioned Cocktail Table | 2006

17 X 50 X 30 INCHES (43.2 X 127 X 76.2 CM)
Aluminum, limestone, stainless steel cable,
powder coat
PHOTO BY ARTIST

Graham Campbell

Hill Dancer | 1999

36 X 72 X 16 INCHES (91.4 X 182.9 X 40.6 CM)

Poplar, sycamore, walnut, paint

PHOTOS BY JOHN LUCAS

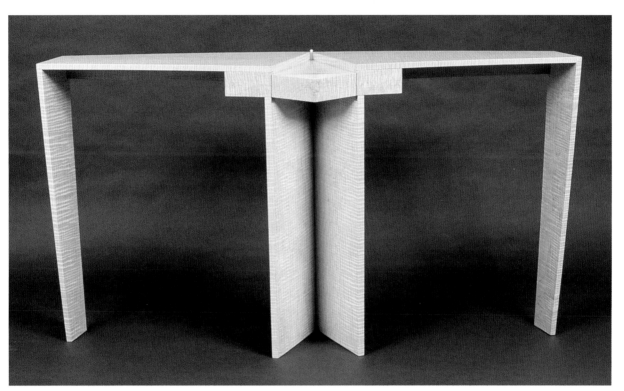

Frederick Puksta

Winged Hall Table | 1987

35 X 56 X 10 INCHES (88.9 X 142.2 X 25.4 CM)

Curly maple, koa, gold leaf, pearl

PHOTOS BY ARTIST

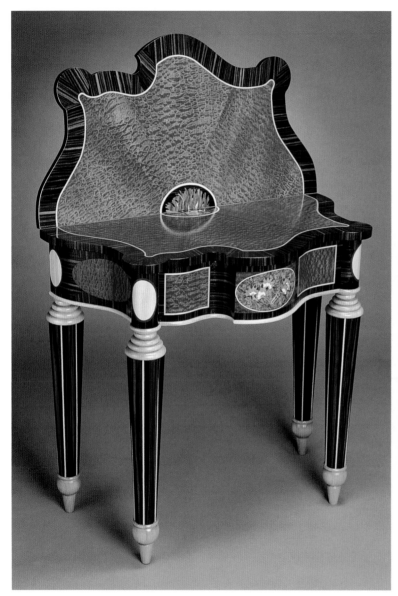

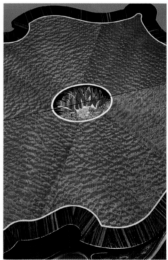

Alfred Sharp
Card Table | 2004

30 X 34 X 17 INCHES (76.2 X 86.4 X 43.2 CM)
Macassar ebony, sapele, sycamore, poplar
PHOTOS BY JOHN LUCAS

Po Shun Leong

Las Vegas | 1999

36 X 54 X 16 INCHES (91.4 X 137.2 X 40.6 CM)

Lacquered maple, bocote, ebony, buckeye burl, wenge, narra, pau amarelo, pink ivory wood, cherry, gold leaf, purpleheart, fiber optic lighting, art glass cubes by Jon Kuhn

PHOTOS BY ARTIST

Yoav S. Liberman

Shah | 2002

18¹/₂ X 13¹/₂ X 10 INCHES (47 X 34.3 X 25.4 CM)

Reclaimed pine, reclaimed heart pine

PHOTOS BY ARTIST

Mervyn L. Krivoshein

Clothespin Table | 2001

57 X 24 X 22 INCHES
(144.8 X 61 X 55.9 CM)

Oak, spruce, mild steel,
copper, Danish oil

PHOTO BY LOUISE FISHER

Michael C. Fortune

Conference Table | 1997

29 X 168 INCHES (73.7 X 426.7 CM)
Cherry, aluminum, hollow core
PHOTO BY ARTIST

Phillip Tennant

Sideboard Table with Drawers | 2004

34 X 64 X 16 INCHES (86.4 X 162.6 X 40.6 CM)

Bubinga, wenge, mahogany, red granite

PHOTOS BY ARTIST

Seth A. Barrett

Entry Table with Three Drawers: Ode to My Thief | 2000

37 X 31 X 17 INCHES (94 X 78.7 X 43.2 CM)

Mahogany, purpleheart, wenge, ash, oak, oil pigment, aniline dye, oil, lacquer

PHOTO BY FRANK IANNOTTI

Lawrence Godfried

Deco Console | 1989

31 X 42 X 16 INCHES (78.7 X 106.7 X 40.6 CM)

Polished marble aggregates, colored cement, marble dust, red oak

PHOTO BY ARTIST

Carter Jason Sio

Quaker Meeting House Table | 1994

30 X 50 X 22 INCHES (76.2 X 127 X 55.9 CM)

Mahogany

PHOTO BY ARTIST

Brian A. Hubel

Slim | 2007

36 X 50 X 14 INCHES (91.4 X 127 X 35.6 CM)
Russian olive, claro walnut, ebony, ebonized ash
PHOTOS BY DON JONES

Carter Jason Sio

Buffet | 1984

30 X 14 X 48 INCHES (76.2 X 35.6 X 121.9 CM)
Benin and purpleheart veneer
PHOTO BY ARTIST

Arnold d'Epagnier

Writing Table | 1990

30 X 54 X 22 INCHES (76.2 X 137.2 X 55.9 CM)

Bubinga, ebony

PHOTO BY MICHAEL LATIL

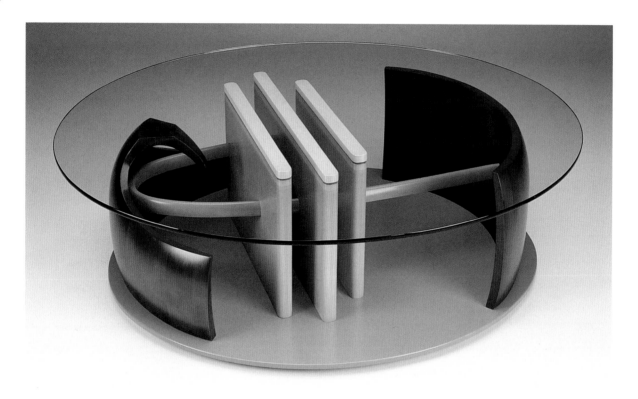

Jennifer E. Schwarz

Gibson's Table | 1988

15 X 56 X 48 INCHES (38.1 X 142.2 X 121.9 CM)

Alder, maple, medium-density fiberboard, colored lacquer, glass

PHOTO BY DAVID BROWNE

Richard Bronk

Untitled | 2006

18 X 48 X 24 INCHES (45.7 X 121.9 X 61 CM)

Cherry, spalted birch, curly maple, wenge, glass top

PHOTO BY WILLIAM LEMKE

Craig Thibodeau

Bubinga Coffee Table | 2005

17 X 42 X 34 INCHES (43.2 X 106.7 X 86.4 CM)

Bubinga, wenge, jatoba, mahogany,
polyester and conversion varnish finish

PHOTO BY CRAIG CARLSON

Kimberly Winkle

Fringed End Table | 2007

22 X 16 X 16 INCHES (55.9 X 40.6 X 40.6 CM)

Polychrome poplar, mahogany, natural
bristles, silver graphite

PHOTOS BY JOHN LUCAS

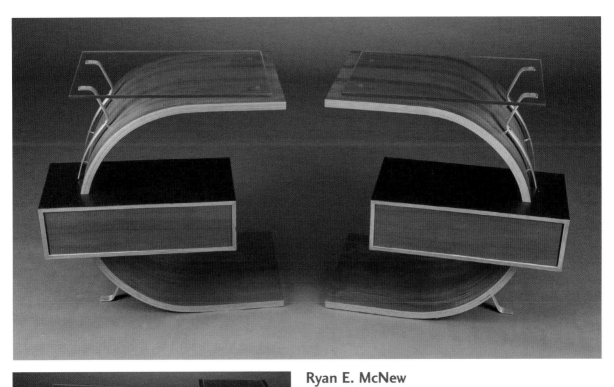

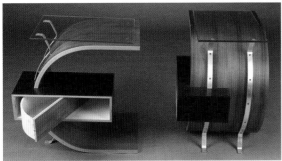

Ryan E. McNew

Curves with Corners | 2006

26 X 29 X 19 INCHES (66 X 73.7 X 48.3 CM)

Plywood, aluminum, glass, teak veneer

PHOTOS BY ARTIST

Trenton Baylor

Bush | 2005

32 X 60 X 28 INCHES (81.3 X 152.4 X 71.1 CM)

Cast bronze, walnut

PHOTO BY DON LINTNER

Dale Lewis

Pursuing the Elusive Red Dot | 2002

24 X 24 X 14 INCHES (61 X 61 X 35.6 CM)
Curly maple, ebony, bloodwood, lacquer finish
PHOTO BY ARTIST

Cameron Van Dyke

Fizz Table | 2006

12 X 82 X 21 INCHES (30.5 X 208.3 X 53.3 CM)
African mahogany, steel
PHOTOS BY SHIPPERT PHOTOGRAPHY

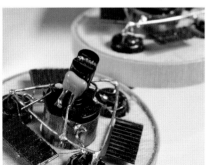

Matthew G. Hebert

Vehicle #1: Table (for Valentino Braitenberg) | 2007

12 X 36 X 36 INCHES (30.5 X 91.4 X 91.4 CM)

Plywood, glass, electronics, milk paint

PHOTOS BY LARRY STANLEY

Sabiha Mujtaba

A Basket of Snakes | 1993

30 X 72 X 42 INCHES (76.2 X 182.9 X 106.7 CM)

Curly maple, rope

PHOTOS BY KURT FISHER

David Trubridge

Offering V | 1996

39³/₈ X 23⁵/₈ X 11¹³/₁₆ INCHES (100 X 60 X 30 CM)

Split oak

Brian Fireman

Heron Table | 2005

37 X 25 X 15 INCHES
(94 X 63.5 X 38.1 CM)

Cherry, crotch cherry

Craig A. Siebeneck

Curve | 2006

35 X 22 X 21 INCHES (88.9 X 55.9 X 53.3 CM)

Walnut, poplar, stainless steel, boiled linseed oil, wax

PHOTOS BY CHRISTINE VERHOFF-SIEBENECK

Mark S. Levin

Pear Coffee Table with Drawer | 2007

16 X 43 X 30 INCHES (40.6 X 109.2 X 76.2 CM)

Australian lacewood, bubinga

PHOTO BY MARGOT GEIST

Sabiha Mujtaba

Serpientes y Monstera | 1999

17 X 42 X 20 INCHES (43.2 X 106.7 X 50.8 CM)
Cherry, curly maple, glass
PHOTOS BY KURT FISHER

Pat Morrow

Leaf Table | 2006

32 X 52 X 14 INCHES (81.3 X 132.1 X 35.6 CM)

Butternut

PHOTOS BY TOBY THREADGILL

Keith Kaar Clayton

150 Sheets | 2000

17 X 38 X 25 INCHES (43.2 X 96.5 X 63.5 CM)

Paper, stainless steel, wenge, aluminum

PHOTO BY JERRY W. COX

John Grew Sheridan

Arachnid Kitchen Prep Table | 2003

37 X 43 X 30 INCHES (94 X 109.2 X 76.2 CM)

Steel, maple

PHOTO BY SCHOPPLEIN.COM

Michael Martell
Claudia Zeber-Martell

Side Table | 2007

24 X 17 X 12 INCHES (61 X 43.2 X 30.5 CM)

Wheel-thrown ceramic base, airbrushed underglazes, gloss glaze finish, glass, brushed aluminum fittings

PHOTO BY JIM MARTIN

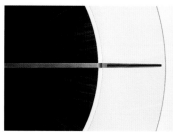

Paul M. Minniti

M Power | 2002

16 X 44 X 44 INCHES (40.6 X 111.8 X 111.8 CM)

Macassar ebony, aluminum, stainless steel, glass

PHOTOS BY SAVANNAH COLLEGE OF ART AND DESIGN PHOTOGRAPHY

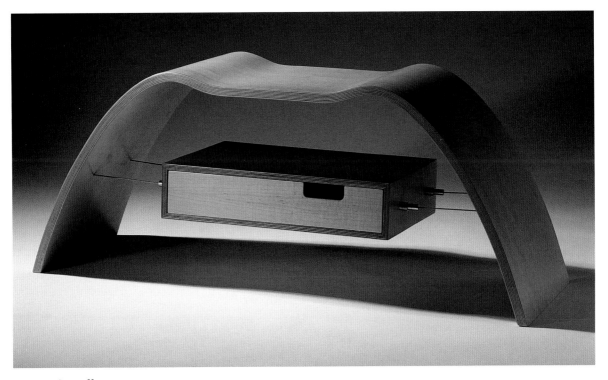

Tyson Atwell

Seismic V1 | 2002

18 X 44 X 16 INCHES (45.7 X 111.8 X 40.6 CM)
Laminated plywood, maple veneer, sterling silver
aircraft cable, sterling silver hardware
PHOTO BY KALLAN NISHIMOTO

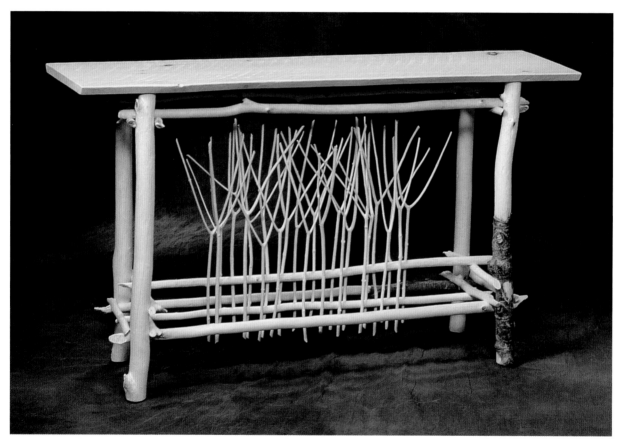

Leonard Fieber

Sweet Sticks Sofa Table | 2006

30 X 53 X 13½ INCHES (76.2 X 134.6 X 34.3 CM)

Aspen, maple, pine

PHOTO BY DAN WHITE

Bob Marsh

Perch II | 2007

23 X 19 X 20 INCHES (58.4 X 48.3 X 50.8 CM)

Walnut, cast resin, paint

PHOTO BY ARTIST

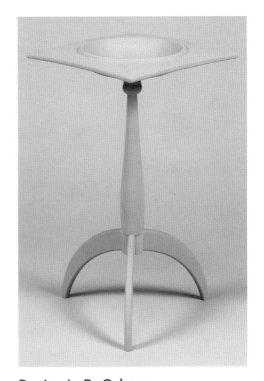

Benjamin R. Osborne

Shaker Birdbath Blue | 2007

25 X 16 X 16 INCHES (63.5 X 40.6 X 40.6 CM)

Poplar, milk paint

PHOTO BY TIM BARNWELL

John Eric Byers

Fountain Table | 2006

15 X 38 X 38 INCHES (38.1 X 96.5 X 96.5 CM)

Mahogany, milk paint, lacquer

PHOTO BY ANDY GILLIS

Richard Bennett

The David Table | 2006

17 X 42 INCHES (43.2 X 106.7 CM)
Polished stainless steel, glass
PHOTO BY CURTIS DROGMILLER

Gareth James Brown

Table Number Two | 2008

28³/₄ X 45¹/₄ X 86¹/₂ INCHES (73 X 115 X 220 CM)

Mahogany, American walnut, New Zealand rimu, aluminum, medium-density fiberboard, white lacquer

PHOTOS BY GRANT HANCOCK

Melissa Morrow

Charm | 2007

17 X 20 X 20 INCHES (43.2 X 50.8 X 50.8 CM)
Cherry veneer, plywood, polystyrene, aluminum
PHOTO BY ARTIST

Christopher Poehlmann

Facet Table | 2000

36 X 48 X 18 INCHES (91.4 X 121.9 X 45.7 CM)
Aluminum, striped oak veneer
PHOTO BY ED CHAPPELL

Mark C. Foehl

Untitled | 2008

29 1/2 X 41 1/2 INCHES (74.9 X 105.4 CM)

Cherry, ash, medium-density fiberboard

PHOTO BY JIM DUGAN

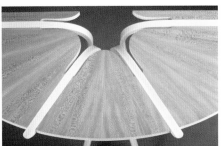

Mason B. McBrien

Lignum Aquatica | 2008

32 X 52 X 20 INCHES (81.3 X 132.1 X 50.8 CM)

Ash, American sycamore, shellac

PHOTOS BY JIM DUGAN

Alexandra Geske

Coffee Table | 2006

18 X 48 X 22 INCHES (45.7 X 121.9 X 55.9 CM)

Medium-density fiberboard, paint, graphite

PHOTO BY TOM MILLS

Jason Schneider
Pedestal Table | 2007

27 X 17 INCHES (68.6 X 43.2 CM)
Walnut, milk paint
PHOTO BY ARTIST

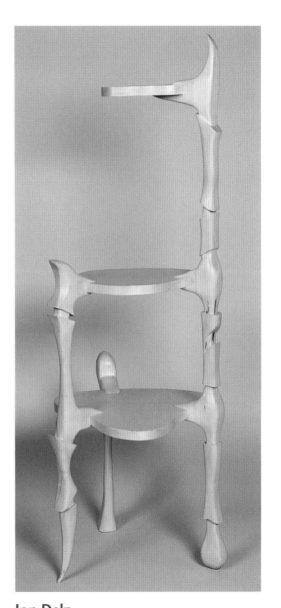

Jon Delp
Three-Tier Table | 2006

48 X 19 X 19 INCHES (121.9 X 48 X 48 CM)
Maple, medium-density fiberboard, maple veneer
PHOTO BY ARTIST

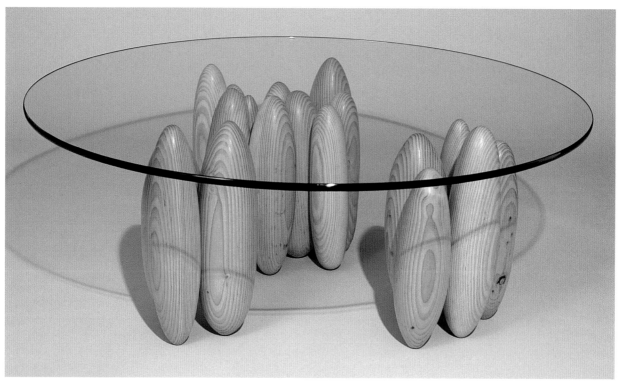

Peter Loh

Clutch | 2005

16 X 44 X 44 INCHES (40.6 X 111.8 X 111.8 CM)

Reclaimed Douglas fir, glass

PHOTOS BY ARTIST

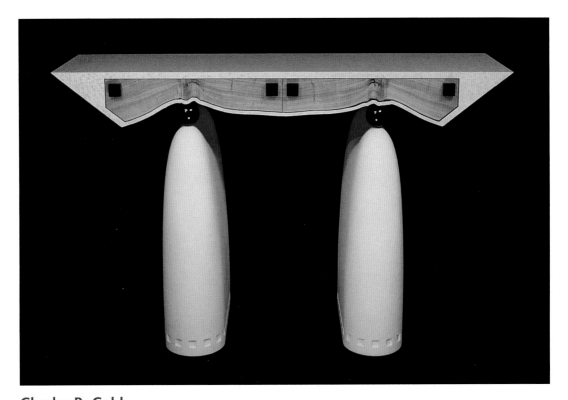

Charles B. Cobb

White Mesa Side Table | 1993

36 X 56 X 20 INCHES (91.4 X 142.2 X 50.8 CM)

Acacia, ebony, alpa veneer, medium-density fiberboard,
latex paint, black lacquer, orange safety paint

PHOTO BY HAP SAKWA

Derek Secor Davis

We All Fall Down | 2000

24 X 30 X 37 INCHES (61 X 76.2 X 94 CM)

Curly maple, poplar, Douglas fir, milk paint

PHOTOS BY JOHN BONATH

Dale Lewis

Voliptuous | 2003

29 X 36 X 25 INCHES (73.7 X 91.4 X 63.5 CM)
Curly maple, cherry, lacquer finish
PHOTOS BY ARTIST

Nicole Jacquard

Mahogany Table | 2000

26 X 24 X 24 INCHES (66 X 61 X 61 CM)

Mahogany, slumped glass, plate glass, rubber

PHOTO BY KEVIN MONTAGUE

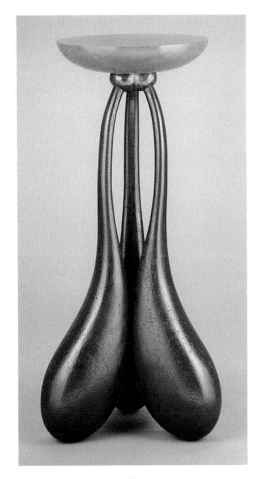

Graham Campbell

Luricka | 2002

34 X 19 X 19 INCHES (86.4 X 48.3 X 48.3 CM)

Poplar, cherry, paint

PHOTO BY JOHN LUCAS

D. Lowell Zercher

Floating Jewel Table | 1989

32 X 26 X 26 INCHES (81.3 X 66 X 66 CM)

Purpleheart, Australian lacewood, cherry, O rings, dye

PHOTO BY DENNIS HELLIWELL

Joe Lastomirsky

Wavy End Tables | 2000

18 X 18 X 18 INCHES (45.7 X 45.7 X 45.7 CM)

Concrete, metal

PHOTO BY MARK HOOPER

Jennifer Costa

It's About Time | 2005

18 X 36 X 20 INCHES (45.7 X 91.4 X 50.8 CM)
Cherry, purpleheart
PHOTO BY ARTIST

Greg B. Smith

Drum Table | 2006

22 X 13 INCHES (55.9 X 33 CM)

Afzelia, canary wood

PHOTOS BY JOHN BIRCHARD

Michael J. Gilmartin

Sextant Table | 1995

28 X 22 INCHES (71.1 X 55.9 CM)

Marine fir plywood, African mahogany

PHOTO BY CHARLEY AKERS

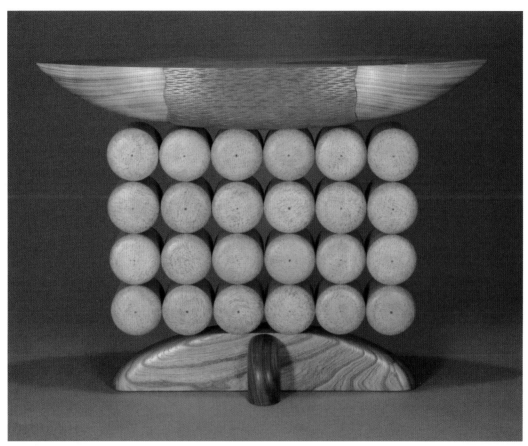

Chris Bowman

Hey Series #1 | 2006

25 X 30 X 8 INCHES (63.5 X 76.2 X 20.3 CM)

Catalpa, poplar, milk paint

PHOTOS BY ARTIST

Katherine L. Martin

Locomotion | 2004

24 X 30 INCHES (61 X 76.2 CM)
Steel, rubber balls, glass
PHOTO BY BRIAN L. MOSHER

Aaron M. Doerder

Collapsible Desk | 2005

29 X 48 X 30 INCHES (73.7 X 121.9 X 76.2 CM)

Sycamore veneer, lacewood veneer, birch plywood,
poplar, poly-mix finish

PHOTOS BY ARTIST

Graham Campbell

Gaming Table | 1989

24 X 20 X 20 INCHES (61 X 50.8 X 50.8 CM)
Birch plywood, poplar, paint
PHOTO BY JOHN LUCAS

Marlene Ferrell Parillo

Nightstand | 2002

28 X 18 X 16 INCHES (71.1 X 45.7 X 40.6 CM)
Ceramic, paint
PHOTO BY HOWARD GOODMAN

Boris Bally

Rectangular Transit Tables | 2006

17½ X 36 X 20 INCHES (44.5 X 91.4 X 50.8 CM)

Recycled aluminum traffic signs, recycled aluminum tube,
steel hardware, champagne corks

PHOTO BY ARTIST

Fred Baier

Tetrahedron and Torroid Table | 1995

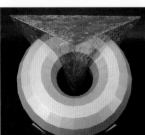

19 11/16 X 19 11/16 X 19 11/16 INCHES (50 X 50 X 50 CM)

Medium-density fiberboard, English oak,
complex polyester lacquer finish

PHOTOS BY LUCY STRACHEN

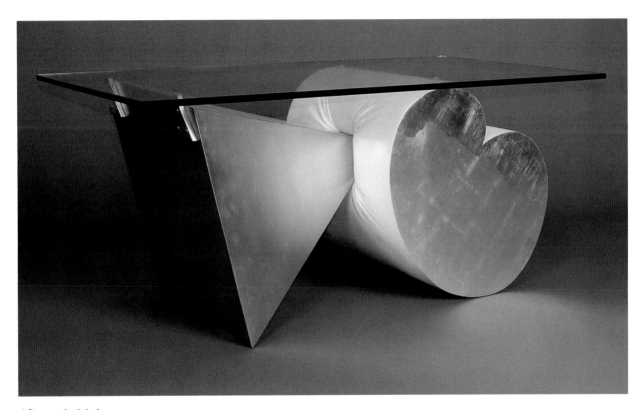

Alison J. McLennan

Purgatory Coffee Table | 2005

19¹/₂ X 46 X 24 INCHES (49.5 X 116.8 X 61 CM)
Plywood, fiberglass, lacquer, 23-karat gold leaf,
silver leaf, 23-karat gold-plated brass

PHOTO BY ARTIST

Alison J. McLennan

Yellow-Legged Table | 2003

21 X 24 X 24 INCHES (53.3 X 61 X 61 CM)

Mahogany, walnut, lacewood, plywood,
fiberglass, lacquer, pigmented epoxy

PHOTO BY ARTIST

Gordon Galenza

Malcolm Tables | 2002

22 X 18 X 18 INCHES
(55.9 X 45.7 X 45.7 CM)

Bubinga, sycamore, zebrano,
anodized aluminum, glass

PHOTO BY JOHN DEAN PHOTOGRAPHS, INC.

Garry Knox Bennett

Tray Table | 2005

23 1/2 X 22 X 14 INCHES (59.7 X 55.9 X 35.6 CM)

Oak, wood, copper, mesh, enamel paint,
acrylic paint, steel

PHOTO BY A.J. MCLENNAN

Greg B. Smith

Entry Table | 2007

32 X 38 X 14 INCHES (81.3 X 96.5 X 35.6 CM)

Moabi, bigleaf maple

PHOTO BY JOHN BIRCHARD

Shaun Fleming

Koa/Marble Foyer Table | 2008

30 X 19 X 46 INCHES (76.2 X 48.3 X 116.8)

Koa, pheasant wood, rainforest marble

PHOTOS BY ROB RATKOWSGI

Cory Robinson

Union Tables | 2007

20 X 22 X 18 INCHES (50.8 X 55.9 X 45.7 CM)

White pine, white oak, mahogany, branches, dye, paint, wax

PHOTOS BY ARTIST

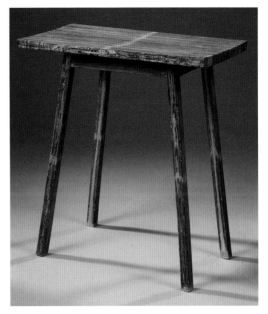

Naushon Hale

Newspaper Table | 2006

12 X 20 X 22 INCHES (30.5 X 50.8 X 55.9 CM)
Newspaper
PHOTO BY MARK JOHNSTON

Lee W. Badger

Stone-Top Table | 2007

18 X 24 X 18 INCHES (45.7 X 61 X 45.7 CM)
Steel bar, angle iron, gun blue finish, Pennsylvania flagstone
PHOTO BY RODNEY LEE GIBBONS

Laura Rittenhouse

Table/Chair | 1999

19 X 22 X 22 INCHES (48.3 X 55.9 X 55.9 CM)

Makore

PHOTOS BY DAVID HAYASHIDA

Carter Jason Sio

Coffee Table | 2005

18 X 42 X 22 INCHES (45.7 X 106.7 X 55.9 CM)

Brown ash, bamboo

PHOTO BY ARTIST

Kevin-Louis Barton

Mondrian II Table | 2003

18 X 46 X 30 INCHES (45.7 X 116.8 X 76.2 CM)

Walnut ply, fabric, foam, fiberfill

PHOTO BY ARTIST

Yang-Jun Kwon

Contrast II | 1993

31 X 24 X 26 INCHES (78.7 X 61 X 66 CM)
Maple, curly maple, leather, dye
PHOTO BY ARTIST

Christopher Poehlmann

Deconstructed Rustic Occasional Table | 1999

30 X 14 X 14 INCHES (76.2 X 35.6 X 35.6 CM)
Solid steel, embossed wood bark, glass
PHOTO BY ED CHAPPELL

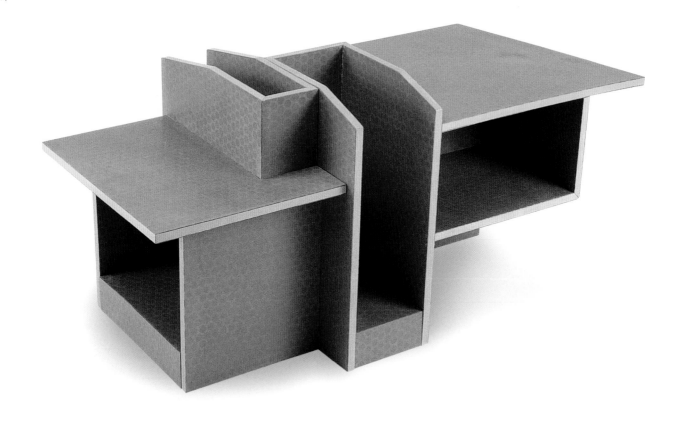

Janice C. Smith

Honey | 1996

21 X 48 X 20 INCHES (53.3 X 121.9 X 50.8 CM)

Honeycomb panel made from recycled paper, ash

PHOTO BY JANICE SMITH

Kevin P. Rodel

Cube Table | 2000

24 X 28 X 28 INCHES (61 X 71.1 X 71.1 CM)

Fumed white oak, tiles

PHOTOS BY DENNIS GRIGGS

Richard Bennett

Dolphin Table | 2001

18 X 80 X 42 INCHES (45.7 X 203.2 X 106.7 CM)

Powder-coated steel, polished stainless steel, glass

PHOTO BY CURTIS DROGMILLER

David O. Wade

*Walnut Natural-Edged
End Table* | 2005

24 X 32 X 26 INCHES (61 X 81.3 X 66 CM)
Walnut, ebonized walnut
PHOTO BY ARTIST

Katherine Ortega

Coffee Table | 2005

14¹/₂ X 31 INCHES (36.8 X 78.7 CM)
Mahogany, glass beads, silver screw eyes, glass
PHOTOS BY RESOLUSEAN

Logan Hirsh

Adjustable Appendage Table | 2007

24 X 12 X 5 INCHES (61 X 30.5 X 12.7 CM)

Forged steel, pine

PHOTO BY ADAM HAWK

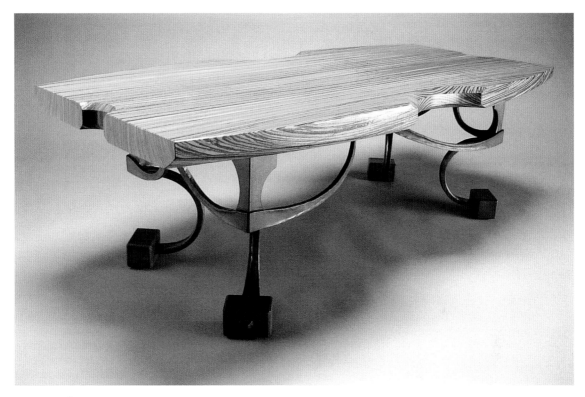

Greg Gehner

Zebrawood Coffee Table | 2006

16 X 24 X 48 INCHES (40.6 X 61 X 121.9 CM)

Steel, zebrawood

PHOTO BY ARTIST

Brian L. Sargent

Turtle Table | 2002

17 X 36 X 24 INCHES (43.2 X 91.4 X 61 CM)
Morado, curly maple, figured maple veneer, glass
PHOTO BY CHARLEY FREIBERG

Thomas Hucker

Low Table | 2007

16 X 18 X 84 INCHES (40.6 X 45.7 X 213.4 CM)
Koa, bronze
PHOTOS BY LYTON GARDNER

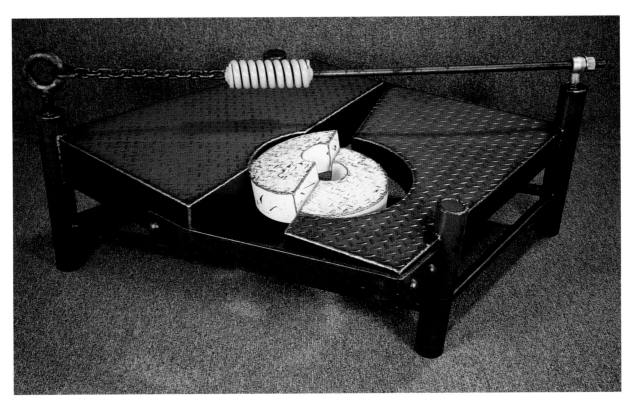

Dale J. Wedig

Split Slab | 2000

16 X 48 X 48 INCHES (40.6 X 121.9 X 121.9 CM)

Steel

PHOTO BY ARTIST

Bailey Humbert Heck

Low Jack Table | 2003

18 X 18 X 74 INCHES (45.7 X 45.7 X 188 CM)
Solid American black walnut, stainless steel,
clear tempered float glass

PHOTO BY ARTIST

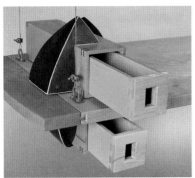

Alexandra Geske

Hanging Desk | 2005

12 X 60 X 24 INCHES (30.5 X 152.4 X 61 CM)
Cherry, basswood, ebony, leather, steel
PHOTOS BY ARTIST

Chanin Cook

Marti | 2003

36 X 60 X 20 INCHES (91.4 X 152.4 X 50.8 CM)

Petrified wood, steel, acid patinas, clear coat

PHOTO BY HAP SAKWA

Carol Russell

Table with Arc Legs | 2006

30 X 25 X 19 INCHES (76.2 X 63.5 X 48.3 CM)
Walnut, cherry, steel
PHOTO BY ROSS HILMOE

Alison J. McLennan

Modern Hoop Hall Table | 2005

45 X 30 X 16 INCHES (114.3 X 76.2 X 40.6 CM)
Mahogany, redwood, foam, fiberglass, plywood,
copper, glass, lacquer, oil paint
PHOTO BY ARTIST

Jere Osgood

Layton Table | 1998

21 ¹/₂ X 24¹/₂ X 14 INCHES (54.6 X 62.2 X 35.6 CM)

Claro walnut, ash

PHOTO BY DEAN POWELL

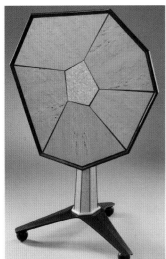

Chris Martin

Tilt-Top Tea Tables | 2007

EACH, 32 X 34 X 34 INCHES (81.3 X 86.4 X 86.4 CM)

Carbon fiber, bird's-eye maple, pearloid, aluminum,
mahogany, bronze, curly white oak, tortoise shell pearloid

PHOTOS BY GEORGE ENSLEY

Michael Gloor

Bot Table | 2005

18 X 18 X 54 INCHES (45.7 X 45.7 X 137.2 CM)

Walnut, Douglas fir

PHOTO BY DAVID GILSTEIN

Mark S. Levin
Vivaldi Leaf Hall Table | 2007

30 X 54 X 26 INCHES (76.2 X 137.2 X 66 CM)
Solid walnut
PHOTO BY MARGOT GEIST

Matthew Bostick
Oak Crotch Table | 2003

18 X 44¹/₂ X 22 INCHES (45.7 X 113 X 55.9 CM)
Red oak, birch
PHOTO BY ARTIST

Brent Harrison Skidmore

Dining Boulder Stack with Swoop | 2007

35 X 80 X 42 INCHES (88.9 X 203.2 X 106.7 CM)

Basswood, mahogany, steel, acrylic paint, glass

PHOTOS BY PETER MCDANIELS

Adrien Rutigliano Segal

Tidal Datum Tables, Verified Water Level: San Francisco, CA
2006/04/27–2006/05/24 | 2007

18 X 18 X 72 INCHES (45.7 X 45.7 X 182.9 CM)

Walnut, steel, hardware

PHOTO BY DANIEL LORENZE

Cale D. Caboth

Cantilevered Writing Table | 2008

36 X 60 X 32 INCHES (91.4 X 152.4 X 81.3 CM)

Ebony, African mahogany, leather

PHOTO BY JIM DUGAN

Danny Kamerath

Evelyn #4 | 2003

25 X 11 ½ X 11 ½ INCHES (63.5 X 29.2 X 29.2 CM)

Bubinga

PHOTO BY JIM OLVERA

Masafumi Sawada

Caddis | 1988

27⁹/₁₆ X 70³/₄ X 23⁵/₈ INCHES (70 X 180 X 60 CM)

Soft iron, walnut

PHOTO BY TETUZO AKASAKA

Phillip Tennant

Long Entry Table | 2006

34 X 110 X 22 INCHES (86.4 X 279.4 X 55.9 CM)
Bubinga, wenge, mahogany, black granite
PHOTOS BY ARTIST

John E. Morel

Kevazinga Low Table | 2006

18 X 30 X 60 INCHES (45.7 X 76.2 X 152.4 CM)

Kevazinga, bubinga, birch, holly

PHOTO BY MATHEW SPIDELL

John McDermott

Coffee Table | 2000

17 X 26 X 52 INCHES
(43.2 X 66 X 132.1 CM)

White oak, glass, copper

PHOTO BY MARTIN FOX

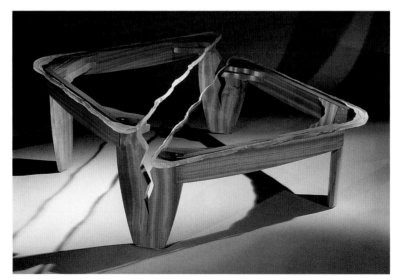

Jay Younger

After Quake | 2004

18 X 38 X 38 INCHES
(45.7 X 96.5 X 96.5 CM)

Sapele, glass

PHOTO BY ARTIST

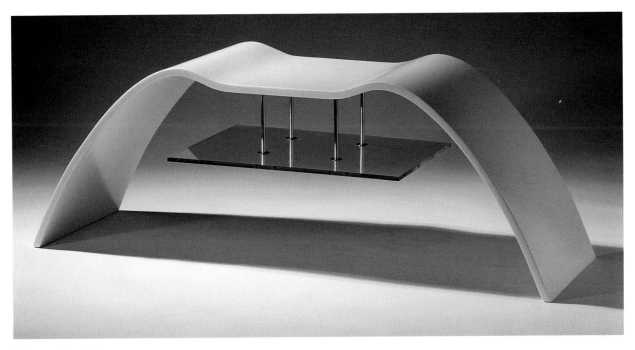

Tyson Atwell

Seismic V2 | 2002

18 X 48 X 16 INCHES (45.7 X 121.9 X 40.6 CM)

Laminated plywood, sterling silver hardware,
acrylic plastic, white lacquer

PHOTO BY KALLAN NISHIMOTO

Garry Knox Bennett

Hall Table and Chair #1 | 2006

37¹/₂ X 31 X 15 INCHES (95.3 X 78.7 X 38.1 CM)

Wood, Thonet café chair, lacquer, aluminum, through-color laminate

PHOTO BY A.J. MCLENNAN

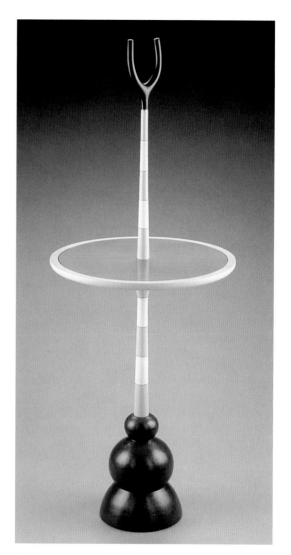

Andy Buck

Wishbone Tea Table | 2001

45 X 18 X 18 INCHES (114.3 X 45.7 X 45.7 CM)

Mahogany, poplar, brass, paint

PHOTO BY BRUCE MILLER

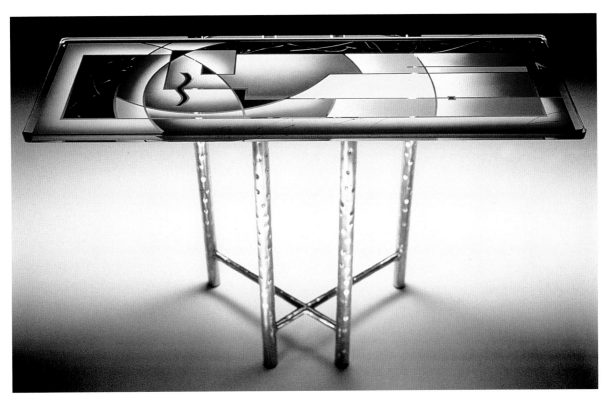

Joan Irving

Journey Entry Table | 2007

16 X 48 X 30 INCHES (40.6 X 121.9 X 76.2 CM)

Glass, metal

PHOTO BY ARTIST

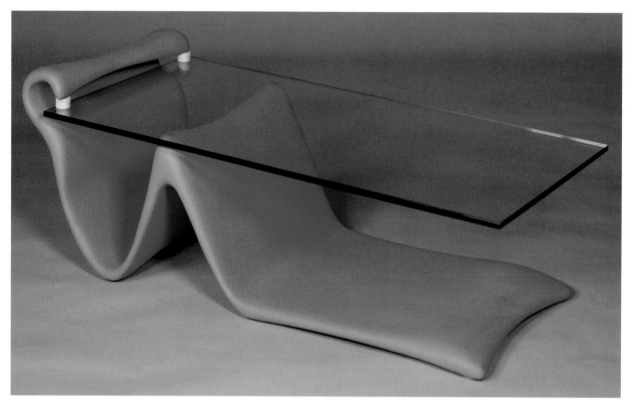

David Hurwitz
Steve Mullenbach
Untitled | 2007

16 X 41 X 20 INCHES (40.6 X 104.1 X 50.8 CM)
Fiberglass, paint, maple, glass
PHOTO BY LUKE BERHOW AND STEVE MULLENBACH

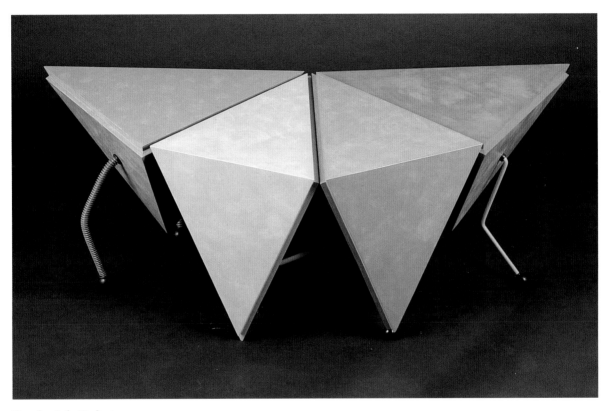

Frederick Puksta

Visitors' Occasional Nesting Tables | 1987

20 X 16 X 19 INCHES (50.8 X 40.6 X 48.3 CM)

Composite board, steel, copper, plastic, paint

PHOTO BY ARTIST

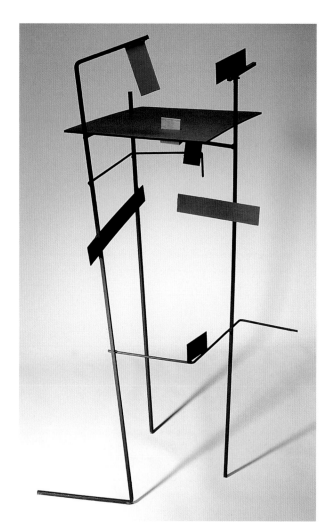

Greg Gehner

Tongue and Groove End Table | 2007

24 X 20 X 20 INCHES (61 X 50.8 X 50.8 CM)

Re-forged pliers, steel, glass

PHOTO BY ARTIST

Genya Glass

Untitled | 2007

31 X 22 X 21 INCHES (78.7 X 55.9 X 53.3 CM)

Metal, acrylics, wood

PHOTO BY ERIC NORBOM

John McDermott

Wheelbarrel Table | 1998

17 X 24 X 65 INCHES (43.2 X 61 X 165.1 CM)

White oak, rubber tire, metal rim

PHOTO BY MARTIN FOX

Sylvie Rosenthal

Birdie Suite | 2007

TABLE, 69 X 34 X 20 INCHES
(175.3 X 86.4 X 50.8 CM);
CHAIR, 19 1/2 X 17 X 15 INCHES
(49.5 X 43.1 X 38.1 CM)

Mahogany, poplar, white oak,
milk paint, steel, mixed media

PHOTO BY STEVE MANN

Gordon Galenza

Reversible Arrival/Departure Station | 2004

72 X 50 X 14 INCHES
(182.9 X 127 X 35.6 CM)

Anigre, maple, paint, mirror

PHOTO BY JOHN DEAN PHOTOGRAPHS, INC.

257

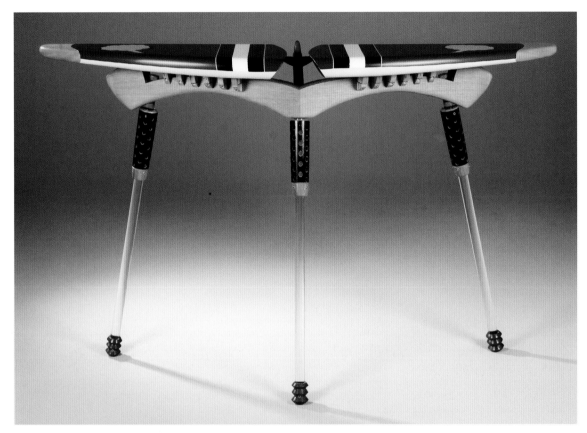

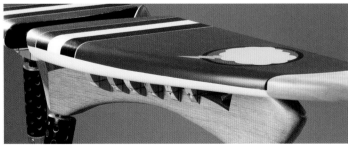

Brad Johns

Attack-A-Loon | 2004

42 X 56 X 18 INCHES (106.7 X 142.2 X 45.7 CM)

Wood, lacquer, stencils, acrylic

PHOTOS BY LARRY STANLEY

Brad Reed Nelson

Stirred, Not Emotionally Shaken | 1998

32 X 14 X 14 INCHES (81.3 X 35.6 X 35.6 CM)
Poplar, steel, glass, paint, touch light
PHOTO BY ALAN MCCOY

Charles F. Heydinger

Gravity | 2007

15¹⁄₂ X 34 X 44 INCHES (39.4 X 86.4 X 111.8 CM)
Baltic birch, holly, glass, steel, powder coat,
acrylic enamel, rubber
PHOTO BY ARTIST

Matt T. Hutton

Core Sample #10 | 2007

29 X 29 X 9 INCHES (73.7 X 73.7 X 22.9 CM)

Ash, fir, ebonized ash

PHOTOS BY JAY YORK

David J. Lunin

WINDsor Table | 2003

25 X 19 X 18 INCHES (63.5 X 48.3 X 45.7 CM)

Sycamore, cherry

PHOTO BY DAVID GENTRY

Paul Lynch

Breakfast Table | 2003

30 X 45 X 32 INCHES
(76.2 X 114.3 X 81.3 CM)

Cherry

PHOTO BY ARTIST

Carl Stammerjohn

Coffee Table | 2000

17 X 47 X 21 INCHES
(43.2 X 119.4 X 53.3 CM)

Fiddleback maple, cherry, acrylic

PHOTO BY MICHAEL J. HENIKA

Tracy A. Fiegl

Fine Dancers | 2007

30 X 38 X 20 INCHES (76.2 X 96.5 X 50.8 CM)

Curly ash veneer, pomele sapele veneer, mahogany, curly maple

PHOTOS BY ARTIST

Hank Holzer

Akira Table | 2006

42 X 72 X 29 INCHES (106.7 X 182.9 X 73.7 CM)
Cherry, bubinga, glass insert
PHOTOS BY ROBERT MCRORY

Angus Ross

Boulder Table | 2005

86½ X 55⅛ X 29½ INCHES (220 X 140 X 75 CM)

Oak

PHOTO BY ARTIST

Pat Morrow

Cactus Table | 2007

31 X 27¹/₂ X 19 INCHES (78.7 X 69.9 X 48.3 CM)

Catalpa, maple, milk paint

PHOTO BY TOBY THREADGILL

Wayne J. Petrie

Jarrah Hall Table | 2004

28 5/16 X 13 3/4 X 59 1/8 INCHES
(72 X 35 X 150 CM)

Western Australian jarrah

PHOTO BY DAVID SANDISON

Glen Guarino

Geometric Table | 2006

27 X 28 1/2 X 13 1/2 INCHES
(68.6 X 72.4 X 34.3 CM)

Oak

PHOTO BY RICH RUSSO PHOTOGRAPHY

Maggie Birmingham

Table, Cloth | 2002

29 X 22 X 22 INCHES (73.7 X 55.9 X 55.9 CM)

Maple, embroidery thread

PHOTO BY ARTIST

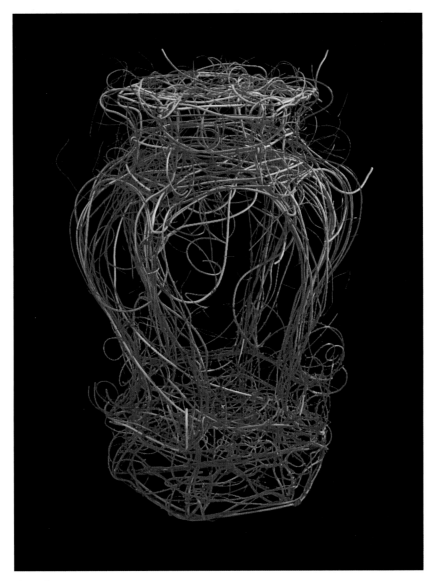

Gord Peteran

Inception Stand | 2004

28 X 20 X 20 INCHES (71.1 X 50.8 X 50.8 CM)

Red electrical wire

PHOTO BY DEAN POWELL

Roy Alan Slamm

Oxalis Writing Table | 1997

30 X 72 X 30 INCHES (76.2 X 182.9 X 76.2 CM)

Old growth white ash, ebonized white ash, pearwood pulls, aniline dye, lacquer finish

PHOTO BY GREGORY MORLEY

Danny Kamerath

Linda | 2005

35 X 13 X 10½ INCHES (88.9 X 33 X 26.7 CM)

Maple, ebony

PHOTO BY JOSEPH SAVANT

Jonathan Edie

Cosmo | 2005

42 X 36 INCHES (106.7 X 91.4 CM)

Ammonite, Chechen, steel, black acid patina, marine-grade clear coat

PHOTO BY HAP SAKWA

Alexandra Snook
Ed Way

Column Table | 2007

30 X 16 X 44 INCHES (76.2 X 40.6 X 111.8 CM)
Cherry, glass, walnut
PHOTO BY ARTIST

John Houck

Conversation Table | 2004

17 X 43 X 63 INCHES (43.2 X 109.2 X 160 CM)

Wenge, zebrawood, mahogany

PHOTO BY ARTIST

David Hurwitz

Arden Writing Desk | 1992

29¹/₂ X 81 X 43 INCHES
(74.9 X 205.7 X 109.2 CM)

Ash, walnut, steel

PHOTO BY ARTIST

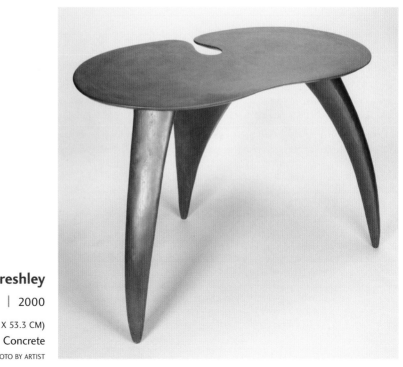

Charles A. Sthreshley

Laptex | 2000

27 X 40 X 21 INCHES (68.6 X 101.6 X 53.3 CM)

Concrete

PHOTO BY ARTIST

Joseph S. Ransmeier

Maple Dining Table | 1999

28 X 48 X 48 INCHES (71.1 X 121.9 X 121.9 CM)

Maple, steel, Danish oil finish, wax

PHOTO BY TIM BARNWELL

John Grew Sheridan

Coopered, Hinged Dining Table | 1983

29 X 42 X 80 INCHES (73.7 X 106.7 X 203.2 CM)

Cherry, brass

PHOTOS BY SCHOPPLEIN.COM

Tony David Kenway

Pede Dining Table | 2005

29$\frac{1}{2}$ X 39$\frac{3}{8}$ X 94$\frac{5}{16}$ INCHES (75 X 100 X 240 CM)

Tasmanian blackwood

PHOTO BY DAVID YOUNG

Aaron C. Fedarko

Cuatro Amigos Table | 2007

30 X 42 X 42 INCHES (76.2 X 106.7 X 106.7 CM)
Cherry
PHOTOS BY JIM DUGAN

William D. Bolstad

Lilac Table | 2006

36 X 42 X 30 INCHES (91.4 X 106.7 X 76.2 CM)

Curly maple, ebonized walnut

PHOTO BY DAN KUITKA

William D. Bolstad

Untitled | 2007

15 X 18 X 36 INCHES (38.1 X 45.7 X 91.4 CM)

Spalted maple burl, African teak

PHOTO BY DANIEL HURST

Brad Reed Nelson

Ann's Table | 2004

17 X 11 X 12 INCHES (43.2 X 27.9 X 30.5 CM)

Reclaimed fur, ebonized mahogany, ceramic vase

PHOTO BY JENNIFER OUTWATER

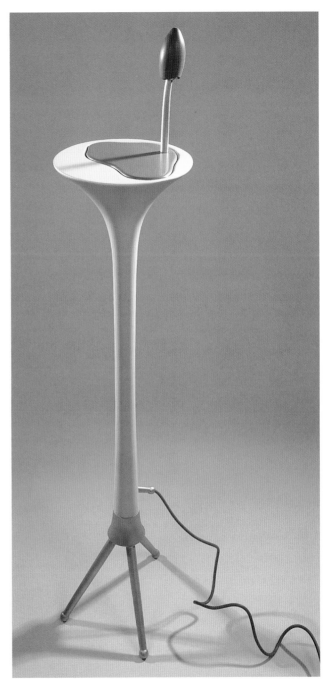

Brad Reed Nelson

Poolside Paradise on a Pedestal | 1998

39 X 9 X 9 INCHES (99.1 X 22.9 X 22.9 CM)

Poplar, aluminum, paint, Osage orange wood,
touch light

PHOTO BY ALAN MCCOY

Brian M. Condran

Crescent Marble Table | 2004

34¹/₂ X 73 X 16 INCHES (87.6 X 185.4 X 40.6 CM)
Black walnut, Mendocino cypress, verde
antique select marble, patinated brass
PHOTO BY ARTIST

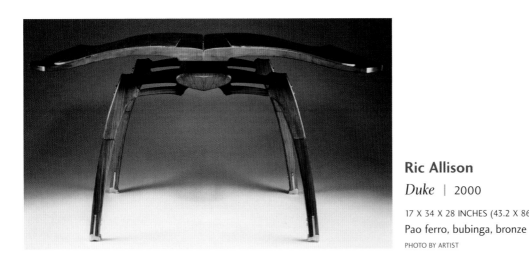

Ric Allison

Duke | 2000

17 X 34 X 28 INCHES (43.2 X 86.4 X 71.1 CM)
Pao ferro, bubinga, bronze
PHOTO BY ARTIST

Matthew Wellman

Shaker Table, Exploded View | 2007

28 X 21 X 25 INCHES (71.1 X 53.4 X 63.5 CM)
Cherry, steel
PHOTOS BY MICHAEL FISKE

David Colwell

GTX Table | 2001

28⁵/₁₆ X 35⁷/₁₆ X 78⁹/₁₆ INCHES (72 X 90 X 200 CM)

Ash, toughened polished glass, rubber suction cups

PHOTO BY ARTIST

Wuthichai Leelavoravong

Add Corner | 2007

18½ X 16 X 16 INCHES (47 X 40.6 X 40.6 CM)

Sepele, white oak

PHOTOS BY WAYNE C. MOORE

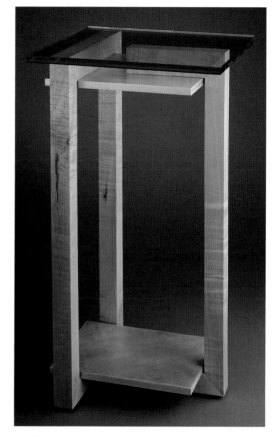

Duncan W. Gowdy

Croze | 2005

45 X 31 X 16 INCHES (114.3 X 78.7 X 40.6 CM)

Maple, brass, stain

PHOTO BY DEAN POWELL

Jeff Johnson

Mate | 1995

30 X 10 X 12 INCHES (76.2 X 25.4 X 30.5 CM)

Figured maple, glass

PHOTO BY AL NOWAK

Robert A. Griffith

Copper-Top Tripod Table | 2005

25 X 16 X 16 INCHES (63.5 X 40.6 X 40.6 CM)

Powder coated steel, copper, glass

PHOTO BY LISA HINKLE

Robb Helmkamp

Slingshot Lady Telephone Table | 2006

37 X 20 X 15 INCHES (94 X 50.8 X 38.1 CM)

Basswood, plywood, acrylic paint

PHOTO BY ARTIST

Lynn Szymanski

Heddle Tables | 2004

21 X 16 X 12 INCHES (53.3 X 40.6 X 30.5 CM)

Basswood, mahogany

PHOTO BY UNH PHOTO SERVICES

Jason Schneider

Intersect | 2003

34 X 40 X 8 INCHES (86.4 X 101.6 X 20.3 CM)

Basswood, milk paint

PHOTO BY ARTIST

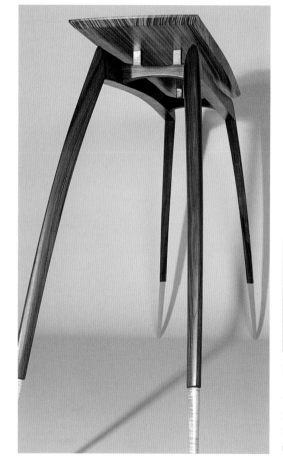

Peter Loh

Recluse | 2004

35 X 66 X 16 INCHES (88.9 X 167.6 X 40.6 CM)

Zebrawood, Bolivian rosewood, maple

PHOTOS BY ARTIST

Michael Puryear

Flatiron Coffee Table | 2001

16 X 48 X 30 INCHES (40.6 X 121.9 X 76.2 CM)

Sycamore, lacewood

PHOTO BY ARTIST

Boykin Pearce Associates

Pool Table | 2001

31 X 102 X 58 INCHES (78.7 X 259.1 X 147.3 CM)

Mahogany, makore, ebony, pool table cloth

PHOTO BY RON RUSCIO

Richard Vaughan

Leonardo Boardroom Table | 2000

28³/₄ X 165 X 59 INCHES (73 X 420 X 150 CM)
Tasmanian blackwood, silver ash, Australian rosewood,
coachwood, hoop pine

PHOTOS BY GREG PIPER

Jere Osgood

Owassa Table | 1998

18 1/2 X 22 X 15 INCHES (47 X 55.9 X 38.1 CM)
Claro walnut
PHOTO BY DEAN POWELL

Burt Levy

Spring Ephemerals Sofa Table | 2006

30 X 18 X 72 INCHES (76.2 X 45.7 X 182.9 CM)
Honduran mahogany, pomele sapele, wenge, satinwood,
anigre, maple, poplar, bubinga, plane tree, walnut
PHOTOS BY ARTIST

Ejler Hjorth-Westh

Game Table | 1998

30 X 54 X 28 INCHES (76.2 X 137.2 X 71.1 CM)

Mahogany, redwood burl, ebony, holly, elm burl, varnish

PHOTO BY KEVIN SHEA

John Clark

Cocktail Table | 2004

20 X 28 X 40 INCHES (50.8 X 71.1 X 101.6 CM)

Mahogany, maple

PHOTO BY TIM BARNWELL

Burt Levy

Gingko Leaf Sofa Table | 2000

30 X 13 X 60 INCHES (76.2 X 33 X 152.4 CM)
Honduran mahogany, pomele sapele
PHOTO BY ARTIST

William J. Wells

Untitled | 2006

24 X 20 X 20 INCHES (61 X 50.8 X 50.8 CM)

Curly maple, Macassar ebony, ebony, abalone shell

PHOTO BY JOANN WELLS

Kerin Lifland

Campodog Tripod Table | 2005

20 X 21 INCHES (50.8 X 53.3 CM)

Walnut, satinwood, madrone burl, maple, cast bronze

PHOTOS BY ZALE RICHARD RUBINS

Craig Nutt

Radish Table | 2004

29 X 24 X 24 INCHES (73.7 X 61 X 61 CM)
Bleached maple, oil paint
PHOTO BY JOHN LUCAS

Bonnie L. Bennett

Big Game | 1999

30 X 36¼ X 36¼ INCHES (76.2 X 92.1 X 92.1 CM)

Birch, mahogany, acrylic stains, permanent markers, colored pencil,
water-based wood finish, stoneware, ceramic glazes

PHOTO BY COURTNEY FRISSE

Gord Peteran

Suspended Table | 2004

42 X 42 X 16 INCHES (106.7 X 106.7 X 40.6 CM)

Fiberglass, brass

PHOTO BY ELAINE BRODIE

Paul Lynch

Franklin Table | 2001

16 X 24 X 48 INCHES (40.6 X 61 X 121.9 CM)

Claro walnut

PHOTO BY ARTIST

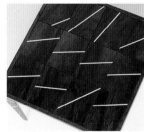

Curt Minier

Side Table | 1987

16 X 17 X 17 INCHES
(40.6 X 43.2 X 43.2 CM)

Walnut, holly

PHOTOS BY GREGG KROGSTAD

Carolyn Grew-Sheridan

*The Difference Between Art and Craft
Is a Matter of Degree* | 1996

20 X 16 X 18 INCHES (50.8 X 40.6 X 45.7 CM)

Sustained yield Mexican rosewood

PHOTO BY SCHOPPLEIN.COM

Adam Hawk
Dan Randall
Aaron Doerder

Collaboration Coffee Table | 2006

18 X 40 X 18 INCHES (45.7 X 101.6 X 45.7 CM)

African mahogany, forged steel

PHOTO BY ADAM HAWK

Richard Judd

Wing Table | 2003

26 X 26 X 26 INCHES (66 X 66 X 66 CM)

Pomele sapele veneer, bending plywood,
poplar, black varnish, glass

PHOTO BY BILL LEMKE

Ted Lott

Walnut Coffee Table | 2005

17 X 48 X 18 INCHES (43.2 X 121.9 X 45.7 CM)

Walnut, wool felt

PHOTO BY TED LOTT

Mark Sfirri

Shaky Ground | 1993

33 X 21 X 13 INCHES (83.8 X 53.3 X 33 CM)
Walnut, cherry
PHOTO BY RANDL BYE

Douglas E. Sigler

End Table/Chopping Table | 2000

36 X 22 X 22 INCHES (91.4 X 55.9 X 55.9 CM)
Cherry, end grain cherry
PHOTOS BY ARTIST

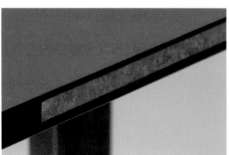

Stefan Furrer

Salamander | 2007

17 X 48 X 21 INCHES (43.2 X 121.9 X 53.3 CM)

Steel, paper-based surface material, linoleum, steel bolts

PHOTOS BY JOHN BIRCHARD

David Trubridge

Offering I—Puahou | 1995

39³/₈ X 23⁵/₈ X 23⁵/₈ INCHES (100 X 60 X 60 CM)

Tanekaha, matai, jarrah pegs, acrylic paint, gold paint

PHOTO BY DAVID EVANS

Chris Bowman

Hey Series #4 | 2008

25 X 20 X 8 INCHES (63.5 X 50.8 X 20.3 CM)

Mahogany, poplar, birch, milk paint

PHOTOS BY ARTIST

Jacque Allen
Ferns and Dots Writing Table | 2007

30 X 36 X 21 INCHES (76.2 X 91.4 X 53.3 CM)
Cherry, basswood, paint, metal and glass knob
PHOTO BY ARTIST

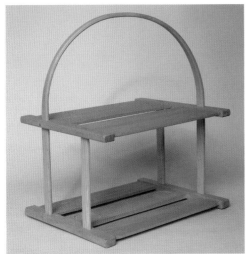

Stefan During
Portable Table | 1995

25⁹/₁₆ X 15³/₄ X 20¹/₁₆ INCHES (65 X 40 X 51 CM)
Elm wood
PHOTOS BY ARTIST

Floyd Gompf

Wheeled Side Table | 2007

29 X 18 X 13 INCHES (73.7 X 45.7 X 33 CM)

Found wood, found wheels

PHOTO BY RICHARD HELLYER

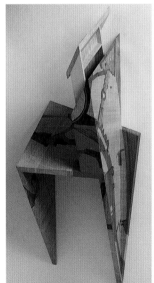

Janice C. Smith

Castle Fly-Over (Wall-Hung Table) | 1993

15 X 37 X 12 INCHES (38.1 X 94 X 30.5 CM)

Anigre, koa, curly and bird's-eye maple veneers, plywood

PHOTOS BY ARTIST

313

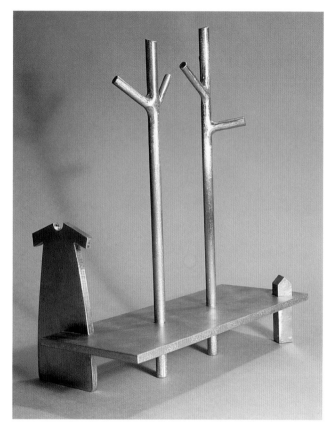

Derek Lance Chalfant

Flowers | 2005

12 X 5 X 10 INCHES (30.5 X 12.7 X 25.4 CM)
Stainless steel
PHOTO BY ARTIST

Jonathan Edie

Larsen Side Table | 2003

24 X 20 X 15 INCHES (61 X 50.8 X 38.1 CM)
Petrified wood, koa, catalox, steel, black acid patina,
marine-grade clear coat
PHOTO BY HAP SAKWA

Michael Gloor

Gazelle Table | 2004

44 X 29 X 9 INCHES (111.8 X 73.7 X 22.9 CM)
Cherry, walnut

PHOTO BY DAVID GILSTEIN

Arnt Arntzen

Stardust Lounge Bar | 2007

40 X 72 X 30 INCHES (101.6 X 182.9 X 76.2 CM)

Walnut, tungsten aluminum helicopter rotor, steel, lacquer

PHOTO BY BRIAN K. SMITH

Joan Irving

Petroglyph Entry Table | 2007

16 X 48 X 30 INCHES (40.6 X 121.9 X 76.2 CM)

Glass, metal

PHOTO BY ARTIST

David Orth

Side Table #7430 | 2006

32½ X 52½ X 16 INCHES (82.6 X 133.4 X 40.6 CM)

Bronze, steel

PHOTOS BY ARTIST

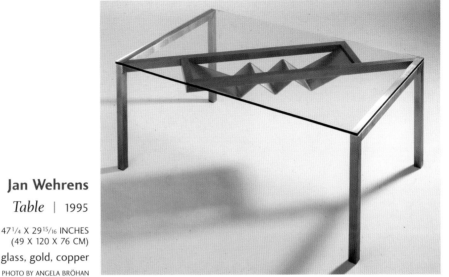

Jan Wehrens

Table | 1995

19 1/4 X 47 1/4 X 29 15/16 INCHES
(49 X 120 X 76 CM)

Steel, glass, gold, copper

PHOTO BY ANGELA BRÖHAN

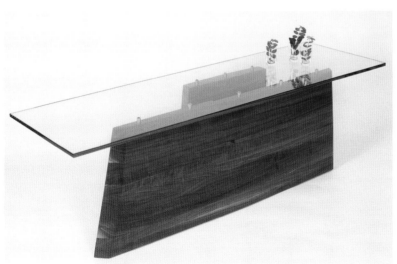

Bailey Humbert Heck

Hansen Table | 2001

15 X 16 X 51 INCHES (38.1 X 40.6 X 129.5 CM)

Solid cherry, solid walnut, solid curly maple,
stainless steel, clear tempered float glass

PHOTOS BY ARTIST

Andy Buck

Side Tables | 2002

30 X 13 X 13 INCHES (76.2 X 33 X 33 CM)

Mahogany, white oak, paint

PHOTO BY BRUCE MILLER

Christopher Green

That Yin-and-Yang Thing | 2008

20 X 18 X 18 INCHES (50.8 X 45.7 X 45.7 CM)

Poplar, birch, acrylic paint

PHOTO BY ARTIST

Seth Rolland

Dreamcatcher Hall Table | 2007

36 X 54 X 15 INCHES (91.4 X 137.2 X 38.1 CM)

Ash, mahogany

PHOTO BY FRANK ROSS

Leonard Fieber

Ahmik's Accent Entry Table | 2007

30 X 35 X 10 INCHES (76.2 X 88.9 X 25.4 CM)

Aspen, maple, pine

PHOTO BY DAN WHITE

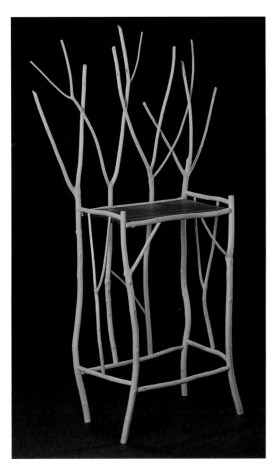

Alan H. Bradstreet

Hall Table for Susan | 1999

59 X 36 X 14 INCHES (149.9 X 91.4 X 35.6 CM)

Ash, cherry

PHOTO BY DENNIS GRIGGS

Gwen H. Granzow

Untitled | 2004

30 X 106 X 46 INCHES (76.2 X 269.2 X 116.8 CM)

Steel, oak, patina, paint

PHOTOS BY PETER HERNANDEZ

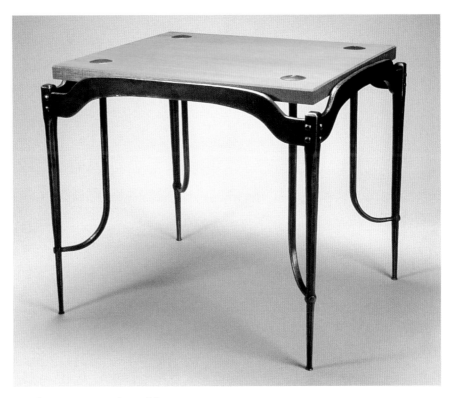

Andrew S. Macdonald

Untitled | 2000

22 X 21 X 24 INCHES (55.9 X 53.3 X 61 CM)

Steel, mahogany wood

PHOTO BY JEFFREY BRUCE

Fletcher Cox

Raw and Cooked #1 | 1995

30 X 26 X 18 INCHES (76.2 X 66 X 45.7 CM)
Cherry
PHOTO BY ARTIST

David Trubridge

Offering III—Figure | 1996

23 5/8 X 23 5/8 X 23 5/8 INCHES (60 X 60 X 60 CM)
Elm, matai, acrylic wash
PHOTO BY DAVID EVANS

Stephen Whittlesey

Eddy | 2006

19 X 72 X 34 INCHES (48.3 X 182.9 X 86.4 CM)

Driftwood, salvaged oak, chestnut

PHOTO BY ARTIST

Sabine Gertraud Rasp

Untitled | 1998

32¹/₂ X 74¹/₂ X 74¹/₂ INCHES (82.6 X 189.2 X 189.2 CM)

Maple, glass, silver leaf

PHOTO BY KAREN BENGALL

Ejler Hjorth-Westh

Shoji Sideboard | 2005

36 X 62 X 18 INCHES (91.4 X 157.5 X 45.7 CM)

Swiss pearwood, linen, French polish

PHOTOS BY JOHN BIRCHARD

Tony David Kenway

Cunji Hall Table | 2006

35⁷/₁₆ X 39³/₈ X 12⁹/₁₆ INCHES (90 X 100 X 32 CM)

Tasmanian huon

PHOTO BY DAVID YOUNG

Erin Dace Behling

Untitled | 2006

65 X 14³/₈ X 22 INCHES
(165.1 X 36.5 X 55.9 CM)

Medium-density overlay,
metal hardware, paint

PHOTOS BY ARTIST

Roy Alan Slamm

Lillian Table | 1997

30 X 72 X 42 INCHES (76.2 X 182.9 X 106.7 CM)

Curly hard maple, ebony and maple rosettes,
walnut inlay, lacquer finish

PHOTO BY GREGORY MORLEY

Farida A. Al Rashaid

I Can't Find My Keys | 2007

32 X 43 X 13 INCHES (81.3 X 109.2 X 33 CM)

Wood, cherry, keys

PHOTOS BY TAYLOR DABNEY

Paul M. Minniti

The Executive | 2000

34 X 68 X 14 INCHES (86.4 X 172.7 X 35.6 CM)

Mahogany, pomele sapele, ebonized mahogany, aluminum

PHOTO BY ROCHESTER INSTITUTE OF TECHNOLOGY PHOTOGRAPHY

Hugh N. Montgomery

Doggett Coffee Table | 2007

17 X 34 X 54 INCHES (43.2 X 86.4 X 137.2 CM)

African mahogany, Western maple burl

PHOTO BY ART GRICE

John E. Morel

Big Bang | 2007

29¹/₂ X 42 X 84 INCHES (74.9 X 106.7 X 213.4 CM)

Honduran mahogany, crotch mahogany, wenge, ebony, mother-of-pearl

PHOTO BY PERRY THOMPSON

Roger Heitzman

Dining Table | 2003

29 X 40 X 84 INCHES (73.7 X 101.6 X 213.4 CM)

Mahogany, wenge

PHOTO BY ARTIST

David Upfill-Brown

Embassy Table | 1998

29 X 60 X 420 INCHES (73.7 X 152.4 X 1066.8 CM)

Australian blackwood, fiberglass, blackwood veneer, plywood

PHOTOS BY ANDREW SIKORSKI

David Fobes

Red, White, Yellow Table | 2003–2006

ON WALL, 44 X 144 X 3 INCHES (111.8 X 365.8 X 7.6 CM)
Mahogany, birch, milk paint, brass
PHOTOS BY WILL GULLETTE

David Barclay

Sofa Table | 2003

28 X 18 X 56 INCHES (71.1 X 45.7 X 142.2 CM)
Wenge, bloodwood
PHOTO BY PETE DIFULVIO

Matt T. Hutton

Core Sample #7 | 2006

34 X 11 X 7 INCHES (86.4 X 27.9 X 17.8 CM)

Walnut

PHOTO BY JAY YORK

Katherine Ortega

Entry Table | 2008

37½ X 43 X 19½ INCHES
(95.3 X 109.2 X 49.5 CM)

Mahogany, glass beads,
silver screw eyes, acrylic

PHOTOS BY RESOLUSEAN

Gary Upton

River Table | 2007

48 X 43 X 12 INCHES (121.9 X 109.2 X 30.5 CM)

Red elm, ceramic cement, copper and iron coating, patinas

PHOTOS BY JIM BECKETT

Ashley Jameson Eriksmoen
Red-Tail Flyer | 2004

36 X 38 X 12 INCHES (91.4 X 96.5 X 30.5 CM)
Mahogany, acrylic paint, milk paint, oil varnish
PHOTOS BY M. LEE FATHERREE

Don Green

Diamond Pattern Coffee Table | 2007

18 X 44 X 24 INCHES (45.7 X 111.8 X 61 CM)

Rosewood, ebonized mahogany, maple

PHOTO BY ARTIST

Michael Regan

Untitled | 2003

31 X 31 X 18 1/4 INCHES (78.7 X 78.7 X 46.4 CM)

Walnut, ash

PHOTO BY ARTIST

Wayne J. Petrie

Out of the Forest | 2005

19 11/16 X 19 11/16 X 19 11/16 INCHES (50 X 50 X 50 CM)

Australian red cedar

PHOTO BY DAVID SANDISON

Donald H. Moss

Blue Mountain Lake Console | 2005

32 X 18 X 55 INCHES (81.3 X 45.7 X 139.7 CM)

White birch, lake stone, black grout, wire

PHOTO BY SCOTT VAN SICKLIN

Natalie Wargin

Woodland Demilune | 2005

45 X 19 X 30 INCHES (114.3 X 48.3 X 76.2 CM)

Newspaper, white glue, wire mesh, acrylic paints, varnish, paper pulp, collaged images

PHOTOS BY PHILIP MROZINSKI

Barry W. Tribble

Foyer Table | 2005

29 X 48 X 22 INCHES (73.7 X 121.9 X 55.9 CM)

Madrone burl, beech, fiddleback English sycamore, pomele sapele,
bee's wing andiroba, dyed pearwood, figured cherry

PHOTO BY ARTIST

John (Jack) Rodie

Atomic Table | 2007

30 X 28 X 28 INCHES (76.2 X 71.1 X 71.1 CM)
Cherry, stainless steel
PHOTO BY ARTIST

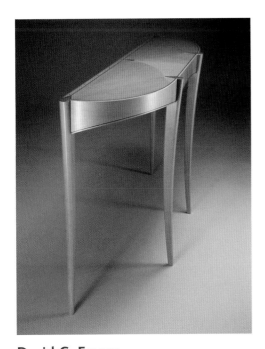

David C. Fraser

Side Table | 1997

31 X 36 X 15 INCHES (78.7 X 91.4 X 38.1 CM)
Hemlock, lacquer
PHOTO BY ARTIST

Steve A. Butler

Sherwood–Coffee Table | 2000

16 X 36 X 36 INCHES (40.6 X 91.4 X 91.4 CM)

Walnut, walnut veneer, aluminum

PHOTO BY ARTIST

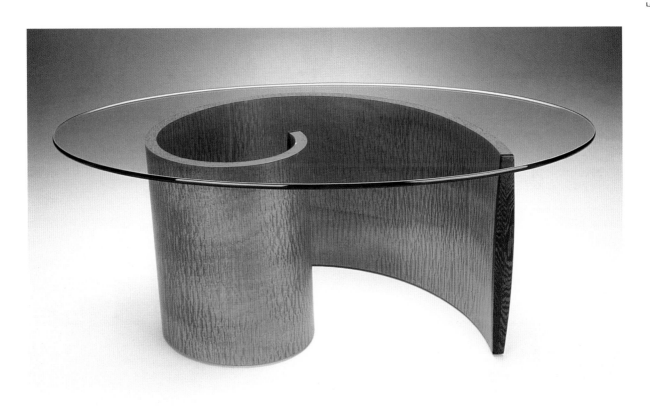

Richard Judd

Spiral Coffee Table | 2001

18 X 50 X 30 INCHES (45.7 X 127 X 76.2 CM)

Pomele sapele veneer, bending plywood, wenge, glass

PHOTO BY BILL LEMKE

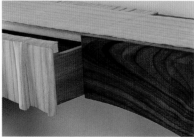

Sabiha Mujtaba

Hall Table with Linen | 2002

36 X 36 X 8 INCHES (91.4 X 91.4 X 20.3 CM)

Walnut, paulownia

PHOTOS BY BART KASTEN

Tracy A. Fiegl
Two-Drawer Hoop Skirt | 2006

35 X 20½ X 17 INCHES (88.9 X 52.1 X 43.2 CM)
English sycamore veneer, ebony veneer, maple,
basswood, ash, milk paint
PHOTO BY ARTIST

Thomas J. Monahan
Unity | 1997

33½ X 18 X 9½ INCHES (85.1 X 45.7 X 24.1 CM)
Ceylon satinwood, wenge, purpleheart
PHOTO BY RON DREASHER

Hugh N. Montgomery

Diamond Series Vase Table | 1996

33 X 12¹/₂ X 17¹/₂ INCHES (83.8 X 31.8 X 44.5 CM)
Cherry, African mahogany
PHOTO BY MARK LAMOREAUX

John Wiggers

Cuff Link Pedestal Table | 2002

19 X 12 INCHES (48.3 X 30.5 CM)
Madero acero, birch plywood,
polished stainless steel
PHOTO BY LORNE CHAPMAN

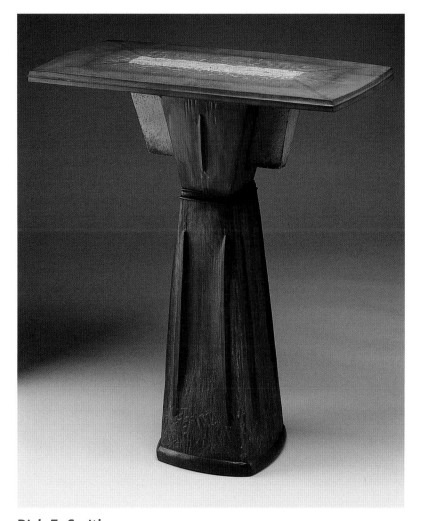

Rick E. Smith

Table | 1995

36 X 40 X 24 INCHES (91.4 X 101.6 X 60.9 CM)

Steel, concrete, rusted surface

PHOTO BY TOM MILLS

John Eric Byers

Diaz Table | 2007

29 X 48 X 84 INCHES (73.7 X 121.9 X 213.4 CM)

Mahogany, milk paint, lacquer

PHOTOS BY ANDY GILLIS

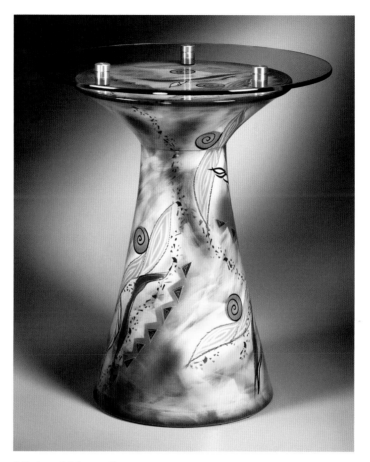

Michael Martell
Claudia Zeber-Martell

Bistro Table | 2007

36 X 32 X 18 INCHES (91.4 X 81.3 X 45.7 CM)
Wheel-thrown earthenware clay, airbrushed underglazes,
gloss glaze finish, glass, brushed aluminum fittings
PHOTO BY JIM MARTIN

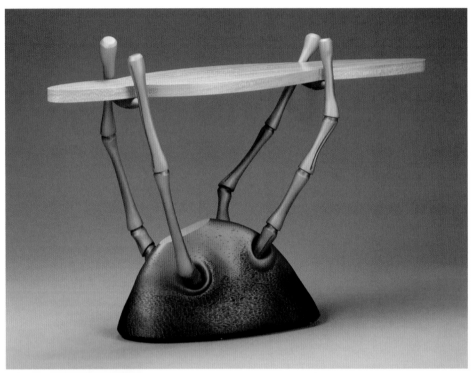

Brent Harrison Skidmore

Top Down Boo | 2003

34 X 57 X 18 INCHES (86.4 X 144.8 X 45.7 CM)

Plane tree, poplar, steel, acrylic paints

PHOTOS BY DAVID RAMSEY

Brian Ferrell
End Table | 2007

20 X 17 X 19 INCHES (50.8 X 43.2 X 48.3 CM)
Maple, padauk
PHOTO BY ARTIST

Chris Bowman
Hey Series #3 | 2006

25 X 28 X 8 INCHES (63.5 X 71.1 X 20.3 CM)
Salvaged Douglas fir, poplar, milk paint
PHOTOS BY ARTIST

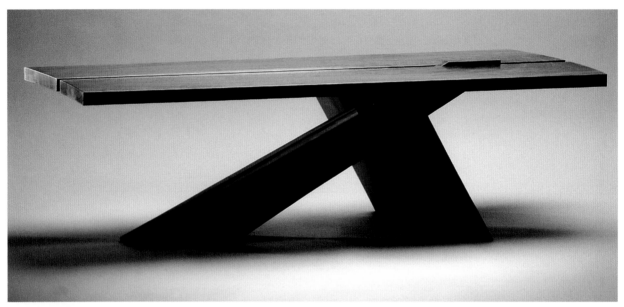

Boykin Pearce Associates

Cantilevered Coffee Table | 2005

18 X 62 X 26 INCHES (45.7 X 157.5 X 66 CM)

Walnut

PHOTOS BY JIM STAYTON

Brian Ferrell

Sideboard Table | 2007

34 X 60 X 17 INCHES (86.4 X 152.4 X 43.2 CM)

Mahogany, stainless steel cable, ebony

PHOTO BY ARTIST

Don Green

Riley Round Table | 2007

27 X 23 X 21 INCHES (68.6 X 58.4 X 53.3 CM)

Mahogany, ebonized mahogany, rosewood, sapele, ebony

PHOTO BY ARTIST

Aaron Levine

Chessellation | 2007

29 X 37 INCHES (73.7 X 94 CM)

Swiss pear, holly, wenge

PHOTOS BY ART GRICE

Douglas E. Sigler

Backgammon Game Table | 2005

30 X 40 X 40 INCHES (76.2 X 101.6 X 101.6 CM)

Walnut, maple, mahogany

PHOTO BY ARTIST

Wesley A. Crosby

Albatross (RTA) | 2001

32$^{1}/_{2}$ X 33 X 9$^{1}/_{2}$ INCHES (82.6 X 83.8 X 24.1 CM)

Ash, stainless steel, blued carbon steel

PHOTO BY ARTIST

Dean Vande Griend

Untitled | 2006

36 X 50 X 19½ INCHES (91.44 X 127 X 49.5 CM)

Maple, bubinga

PHOTO BY GEORGE ENSLEY

Adam D. Fisher

Dovetail Table | 2007

25¹/₂ X 18 X 34¹/₂ INCHES (64.8 X 45.7 X 87.6 CM)

Curly maple, bird's-eye maple, glass

PHOTO BY ARTIST

Robert G. Reid

Walking Tables | 2008

24 X 16 X 17 INCHES (61 X 40.6 X 43.2 CM)
Found tree limbs, poplar, mahogany,
oil finish, latex paint

PHOTO BY ARTIST

Scott Grove

Bob Jr. | 2005

33 X 60 X 12 INCHES (83.8 X 152.4 X 30.5 CM)
Pomele sapele, oak, maple, fiber-reinforced
plastic, copper polychrome

PHOTO BY JOHN SMILLIE

Bob Marsh

Perch I | 2006

120 X 50 X 40 INCHES (304.8 X 127 X 101.6 CM)

Mahogany, cast resin, paint

PHOTO BY ARTIST

Gord Peteran

Assembled Table | 2008

40 X 48 X 18 INCHES (101.6 X 121.9 X 45.7 CM)

Found wood, brass

PHOTOS BY ELAINE BRODIE

Mark Rehmar

Bubinga Leaf Table | 2005

30 X 76 X 44 INCHES (76.2 X 193 X 111.8 CM)

Curly bubinga, ebony, rosewood

PHOTO BY ARTIST

Joe Stearns
Leland Coffee Table | 2002

17 X 46 X 23 INCHES (43.2 X 116.8 X 58.4 CM)
Panga panga, curly cherry veneers
PHOTO BY DAVID SPECKMAN

Joe Stearns
Spence Coffee Table | 2004

17 X 49 X 21 INCHES (43.2 X 124.5 X 53.3 CM)
African mahogany, curly maple, Peruvian walnut
PHOTO BY DAVID SPECKMAN

Stephen Whittlesey

Dreamboat | 2006

20 X 98 X 38 INCHES (50.8 X 248.9 X 96.5 CM)

Oak stem from old fishing boat, salvaged yellow pine

PHOTOS BY ARTIST

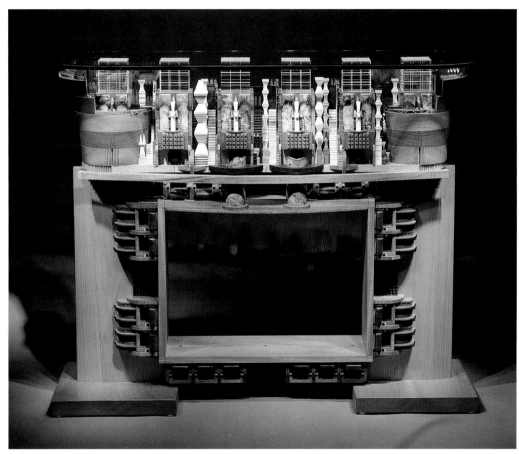

Po Shun Leong

Untitled | 2000

36 X 54 X 16 INCHES (91.4 X 137.2 X 40.6 CM)

Mahogany, wenge, maple, buckeye burl, ebony, glass cubes by Latchezar Boyadjiev, fiber optic lighting

PHOTOS BY ARTIST

Don Green

Ava Console Table | 2007

29 X 54 X 17 INCHES (73.7 X 137.2 X 43.2 CM)

Cherry, avodire, dyed pear

PHOTO BY ARTIST

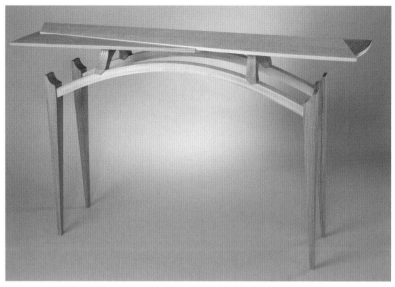

Andrew Aaron Kopp

Two-Tone Mantis | 2007

32 X 56 X 14 INCHES (81.3 X 142.2 X 35.6 CM)
Bird's-eye maple, curly white oak
PHOTOS BY GEORGE ENSLEY

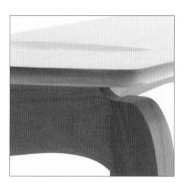

Monika Olejnik

Pod Entrance Table | 2006

32 X 14 X 38 INCHES
(81.3 X 35.6 X 96.5 CM)
Ash
PHOTOS BY ARTIST

Brent Harrison Skidmore

Swell Life with Apple | 2002

35 X 38 X 14 INCHES (88.9 X 96.5 X 35.6 CM)

Maple, basswood, acrylic paint

PHOTO BY DAVID RAMSEY

Mark Zenone

Lemmus | 2006

45 X 24 X 12 INCHES (114.3 X 61 X 30.5 CM)

Quilted makore, curly maple, maple burl, walnut, bubinga

PHOTO BY ANNA S. TAYLOR

Maggie Birmingham

Love's Labor | 2003

30 X 44 X 40 INCHES (76.2 X 111.8 X 101.6 CM)

Walnut, embroidery, milk paint

PHOTO BY JOHN WILSON WHITE

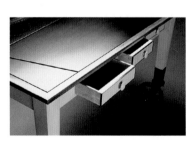

Sylvie Rosenthal

Racing Desk | 2003

30 X 48 X 24 INCHES (76.2 X 121.9 X 61 CM)

Maple, mahogany, poplar, oak, steel, dye, milk paint

PHOTOS BY ARTIST

Brad Smith

Checker Table with Steel Wheel Base | 2007

228 X 23 X 23 INCHES (71.1 X 58.4 X 58.4 CM)
Mixed hardwoods, turned willow post, found steel base

PHOTOS BY JOSH GOLEMAN

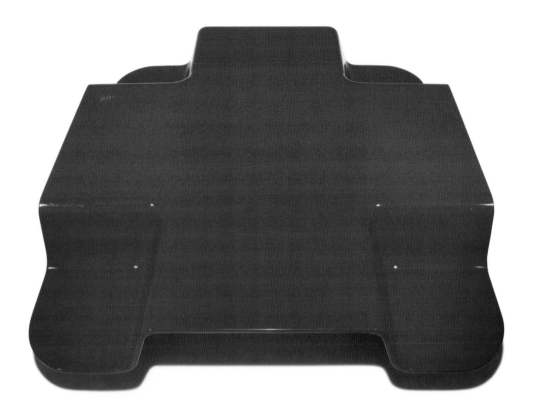

Andrew Clinch
Douglas E. Fanning
Ori | 2001

46 X 46 X 16 INCHES (116.8 X 116.8 X 40.6 CM)
Fiberglass

PHOTOS BY NATHAN SAYERS

Kimberly Winkle

Odd Man Out, Triple-Green Coffee Table | 2007

22 X 50 X 18 INCHES (55.9 X 127 X 45.7 CM)

Polychrome poplar, mahogany, graphite

PHOTO BY JOHN LUCAS

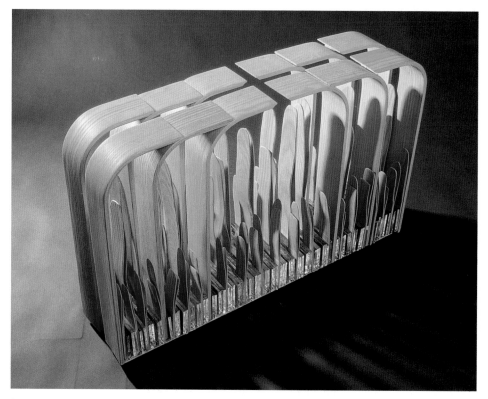

Rosario Mercado

Seaweed | 1995

18³⁄₄ X 30 X 7 INCHES (47.6 X 76.2 X 17.8 CM)

Ash, glass

PHOTO BY ARTIST

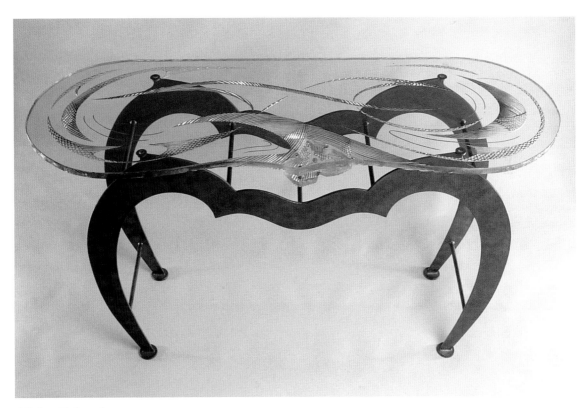

Alisha Volotzky

Bombay | 2004

30 X 58 X 20 INCHES (76.2 X 147.3 X 50.8 CM)

Carved, laminated, and painted glass, powder-coated steel

PHOTO BY PAUL MOSHEY

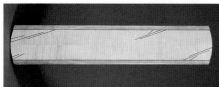

Curt Minier

Entry Table | 1987

35 X 77 X 15 INCHES (88.9 X 195.6 X 38.1 CM)
Maple solids and veneers, cocobolo inlay, paint
PHOTOS BY GREGG KROGSTAD

Mark Rehmar

Console Table | 2003

40 X 48 X 16 INCHES (101.6 X 121.9 X 40.6 CM)
Bubinga, curly maple
PHOTO BY ARTIST

Gord Peteran

A Table Made of Wood | 1999

31 X 38 X 15 INCHES (78.7 X 96.5 X 38.1 CM)

Wood

PHOTO BY ELAINE BRODIE

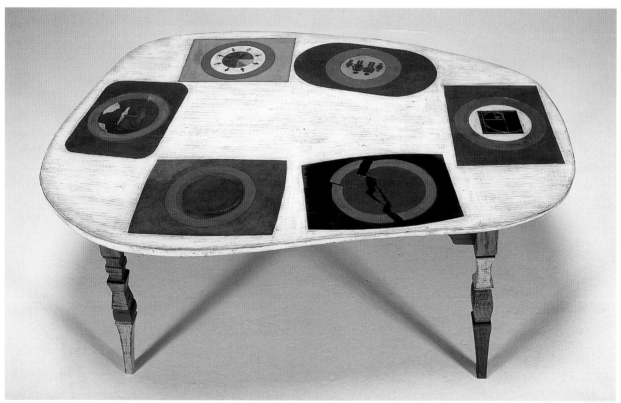

Michael de Forest

The Family | 1998

29 X 63 X 4½ INCHES (73.7 X 160 X 11.4 CM)

Poplar, milk paint

PHOTOS BY PHIL HARRIS

David Fobes

Succulent | 2001

36 X 36 X 28½ INCHES (91.4 X 91.4 X 72.4 CM)
Birch, birch ply, hardware, milk paint, acrylic paint
PHOTOS BY MELINDA HOLDEN

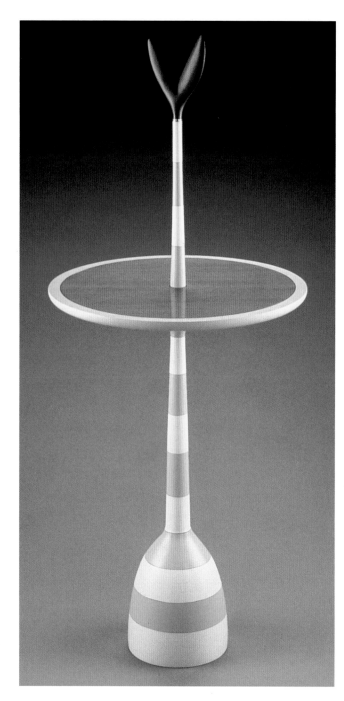

Andy Buck

Green Leaf Tea Table | 2001

46 X 18 X 18 INCHES (116.8 X 45.7 X 45.7 CM)
Mahogany, poplar, brass, paint
PHOTO BY BRUCE MILLER

Seth A. Barrett

Hall Table Structure | 2002

37 X 67 X 20 INCHES (94 X 170.2 X 50.8 CM)

Ash, jatoba, lacquer

PHOTO BY FRANK IANNOTTI

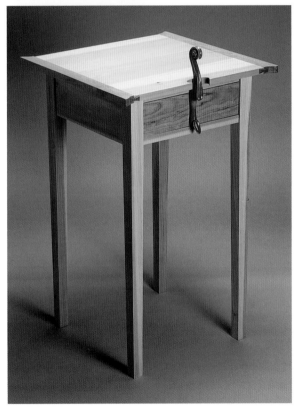

Thomas R. Simpson

Plant Stand | 2006

30¹/₂ X 14 X 14 INCHES (77.5 X 35.6 X 35.6 CM)
Bubinga, polyurethane finish

PHOTO BY MICHAEL WHEATLEY

Yoav S. Liberman

Scott Wiseman's Side Table | 2002

30 X 16 X 16 INCHES (76.2 X 40.6 X 40.6 CM)
Poplar, birch, cherry, spalted poplar, maple, sapele

PHOTOS BY ARTIST

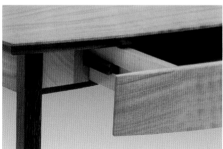

Rob Hare

Entry Table | 1994

35 X 48 X 20 INCHES (88.9 X 121.9 X 50.8 CM)

Figured mahogany, wenge, laminated wenge

PHOTOS BY RALPH GABRINER

Richard Bronk

Untitled | 2004

31 X 47 X 17 INCHES (78.7 X 119.4 X 43.2 CM)

Cherry, curly maple, spalted birch, wenge

PHOTO BY WILLIAM LEMKE

Mats Fogelvik

High Heels | 2005

24 X 24 X 24 INCHES (61 X 61 X 61 CM)
Koa, koa veneer, wenge
PHOTO BY ARTIST

Frances M. Diemoz

Standing Prayer Table | 1998

41 X 96 X 9½ INCHES (104.1 X 243.8 X 24.1 CM)

Curly and bird's-eye hard maple, African weeping wattle, lacquer, Noah bells from recycled metal

PHOTOS BY DEAN POWELL

Nathaniel C. Brown

Untitled | 2004

31 X 27 X 26 INCHES (78.7 X 68.6 X 66 CM)

Ash, oak

PHOTO BY DEAN POWELL

David Simcox

Mells | 2004

17³/₄ X 44³/₄ X 19¹/₂ INCHES (45.1 X 113.7 X 49.5 CM)

Bird's eye maple, yew, maple

PHOTO BY KEITH LEIGHTON

Graham Campbell

Tlali Tlali | 2007

EACH, 32 X 18 X 18 INCHES (81.3 X 45.7 X 45.7 CM)

Poplar, mahogany, paint

PHOTO BY ARTIST

Jere Osgood

Water Table | 2007

25¼ X 15 X 15 INCHES (64.1 X 38.1 X 38.1 CM)

Brazilian tulipwood, wenge

PHOTO BY DEAN POWELL

Chia-Wei Sun

Block | 2007

8 X 7 X 18 INCHES (20.3 X 17.8 X 45.7 CM)

Poplar, red oak, glass

PHOTO BY WAYNE C. MOORE

Janice C. Smith

Untitled | 1984

19 X 22 X 22 INCHES (48.3 X 55.9 X 55.9 CM)

Ash

PHOTO BY ARTIST

Jacob M. Kulin

Coffee Table | 2007

21 X 21 X 50 INCHES (53.3 X 53.3 X 127 CM)
Glass, steel, reclaimed hemlock
PHOTO BY ARTIST

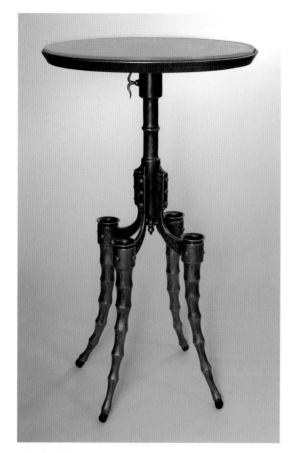

Chris Shea
Arthropod Side Table | 2006

30 X 18 X 18 INCHES (76.2 X 45.7 X 45.7 CM)
Forged steel, cast glass, oil finish
PHOTO BY MELANIE SOTTO

Craig Nutt
Tomato Table | 1996

26 X 23 X 23 INCHES (66 X 58.4 X 58.4 CM)
Dyed and natural wood marquetry, oil paint
PHOTO BY RICKEY YANAURA

Joe Lastomirsky

Split-Level | 1998

17 X 36 X 18 INCHES (43.2 X 91.4 X 45.7 CM)

Concrete, fir

PHOTOS BY MARK HOOPER

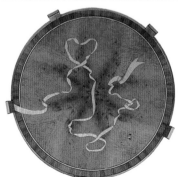

Paul Schürch

Butterfly Ribbon | 1993

19 X 42 INCHES (48.3 X 106.7 CM)

Walnut, madrone, satinwood, lemonwood,
tulip, ebony, lapis lazuli, marble, silver

PHOTOS BY WAYNE MCCALL

Walt Cottingham

Cherry Laurel Table | 2007

30 X 41 X 17 INCHES (76.2 X 104.1 X 43.2 CM)

Cherry, mountain laurel

PHOTO BY PAUL JEREMIAS

Marianne Lattanzio Albanese

Black Walnut Console Table | 2006

36 X 48 X 16 INCHES (91.4 X 121.9 X 40.6 CM)
Black walnut, Italian olivewood, sugar maple, pink ivory
PHOTOS BY GENE SMIRNOV

Roger Heitzman

Coffee Table | 2007

20 X 28 X 28 INCHES (50.8 X 71.1 X 71.1 CM)
Jarrah, pearwood
PHOTO BY ARTIST

Mark Rehmar

Walnut Dining Table | 2006

30 X 58 X 40 INCHES (76.2 X 147.3 X 101.6 CM)

Walnut, ebony, rosewood

PHOTO BY ARTIST

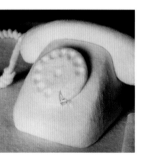

Catherine M. O'Leary

Felt Office | 2006

39³/₈ X 59¹/₁₆ X 78³/₄ INCHES (100 X 150 X 200 CM)

Pine, synthetic hardboard, plastic, stainless steel, merino wool

PHOTOS BY CHRIS FRANKLIN

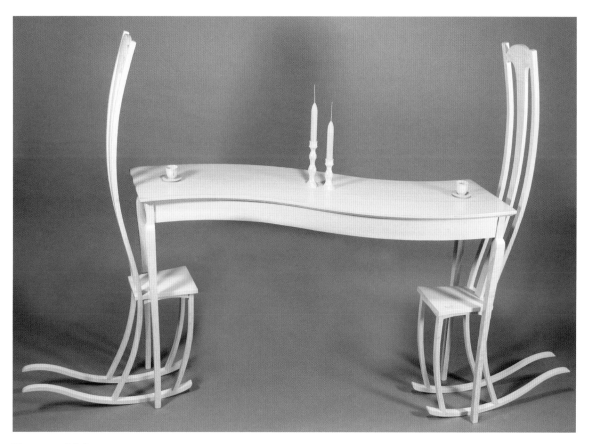

Damon McIntyre

Tea for Two | 2007

42 X 48 X 16 INCHES (106.7 X 121.9 X 40.6 CM)

White oak

PHOTO BY ARTIST

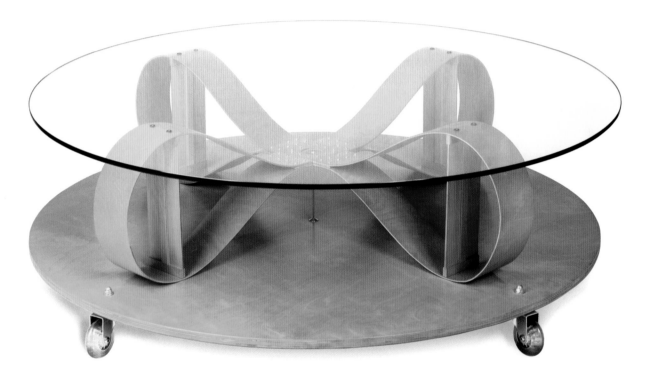

Mordechai Schleifer

Stabila Mobila | 2003

15³/₄ X 47¹/₄ INCHES (40 X 120 CM)
Toned plywood, glass

PHOTO BY YOAV GURIN

Chris Bowman

Hey Series #2 | 2006

25 X 20 X 8 INCHES (63.5 X 50.8 X 20.3 CM)

Mahogany, poplar, milk paint

PHOTO BY ARTIST

Garry Knox Bennett

Hall Table and Chair #2 | 2006

43 X 48¹/₂ X 14 INCHES (109.2 X 123.2 X 35.6 CM)

Oak, chair, pine, enamel paint, lacquer, cotton upholstery

PHOTO BY A.J. MCLENNAN

Craig Thibodeau

Campion Display Table | 2006

31 X 26¹/₂ X 26¹/₂ INCHES (78.7 X 67.3 X 67.3 CM)

Pau ferro, satinwood, holly, poplar, ebony, aluminum, silver, polyester finish

PHOTO BY CRAIG CARLSON

Sam T. Reynolds

Five-Legged Carpinus Table | 2006

21 X 18 X 16 INCHES (53.3 X 45.7 X 40.6 CM)

Hornbeam, mulberry

PHOTO BY JERRY MARKATOS

Jan Huling

Untitled | 2005

23 X 19½ X 20½ INCHES (58.4 X 49.5 X 52.1 CM)

Wood, glass, beads, ball-chain, gems, photograph

PHOTOS BY PHIL HULING

Patrick L. Dougherty

Cosmos Table | 2007

20 X 26½ INCHES (50.8 X 67.3 CM)

Wheel-formed earthenware clay, underglazes, glaze

PHOTO BY JAY BACHEMIN

Garry Knox Bennett

Untitled | 2006

21 X 16¹/₂ X 16¹/₂ INCHES (53.3 X 41.9 X 41.9 CM)

Douglas fir, wood, acrylic paint, lacquer

PHOTO BY A.J. MCLENNAN

Kevin J. Waddell

Get Some Zs | 2005

22 X 16 X 14 INCHES (55.9 X 40.6 X 35.6 CM)

Poplar, paint

PHOTO BY TOM MILLS

About the Juror

Andrew H. Glasgow is the Executive Director of the American Craft Council, the United States' premier craft organization, which publishes *American Craft* magazine and produces the American Craft Shows. Prior to joining the Council, Glasgow was Executive Director of The Furniture Society. He has also held positions at the Southern Highland Craft Guild and Blue Spiral 1 gallery, both in Asheville, North Carolina, as well as at Alabama's Birmingham Museum of Art. He serves on the advisory boards of several museums that specialize in craft, and he is a trustee of the Ogden Museum of Southern Art in New Orleans, Louisiana. Glasgow is a frequent writer, curator, and juror in the craft and decorative-arts fields. He splits his time between Asheville and New York City.

Craig Nutt
Radish Table | 2004

Acknowledgments

I had the pleasure of meeting Andrew Glasgow when he was Executive Director of The Furniture Society in Asheville, North Carolina. I expected he would bring intelligence, sensitivity, and insight to his work as juror, and he succeeded brilliantly in helping shape the book you hold in your hands. I loved having the conscientious, creative Julie Hale as the Production Editor for a book with so many components; she sees problems before they happen and negotiates paths that lead to splendid outcomes. Dawn Dillingham's work with Julie was invaluable, as always, and Nancy Orban also offered production-editorial assistance. Cassie Moore aided me in the book's development with her usual grace. Jackie Kerr brought her artistic eye to the book's layout, and Shannon Yokeley helped direct an art team that included interns Will Ketcham, Nicole Minkin, and Kelly Stallard. Craig Nutt, the juror for the book's wonderful sister volume *500 Chairs*, kindly offered an image of his *Radish Table* for use in our call for entries.

Above all, I wish to acknowledge and thank the skilled furniture artists whose work is featured in these pages, as well as their photographers. We hope you enjoy this beautiful book, which was a labor of love for all involved.

Ray Hemachandra
Senior Editor

Contributing Artists

Al Rashaid, Farida A.
Richmond, Virginia
332

Albanese, Marianne Lattanzio
Worcester, Pennsylvania
119, 402

Allen, Jacque
Asheville, North Carolina
99, 103, 311

Allison, Ric
Narberth, Pennsylvania
79, 283

Arntzen, Arnt
Vancouver, British Columbia, Canada
152, 316

Atwell, Tyson
San Francisco, California
152, 189, 249

Badger, Lee W.
Hedgesville, West Virginia
221

Baier, Fred
Pewsey, Wiltshire, England
65, 67, 214

Bally, Boris
Providence, Rhode Island
113, 213

Barclay, David
Bergen, New York
338

Barrett, Seth A.
Milan, New York
167, 387

Barton, Kevin-Louis
San Francisco, California
78, 224

Baylor, Trenton
Caledonia, Wisconsin
176

Behling, Erin Dace
Indianapolis, Indiana
330

Bennett, Bonnie L.
Beaverton, Oregon
300

Bennett, Garry Knox
Oakland, California
217, 250, 408, 412

Bennett, Richard
Detroit, Michigan
193, 228

Bergsøe, Laura
Hørsholm, Denmark
38

Birmingham, Maggie
Oakland, California
268, 376

Blomenkamp, Kevin Ross
St. Louis, Missouri
155

Bolstad, William D.
Jefferson, Oregon
75, 279

Bossert, Anne
Fort Collins, Colorado
15, 147

Bostick, Matthew
Memphis, Tennessee
241

Bowman, Chris
Indianapolis, Indiana
209, 310, 357, 407

Boykin Pearce Associates
Denver, Colorado
292, 358

Bradstreet, Alan H.
Pownal, Maine
323

Bright, Brian
Randolph Center, Vermont
136

Bronk, Richard
Plymouth, Wisconsin
60, 173, 390

Brown, Gareth James
Adelaide, Australia
148, 194

Brown, Nathaniel C.
Berkeley, California
392

Buck, Andy
Honeoye Falls, New York
250, 320, 386

Butler, Steve A.
Layton, New Jersey
348

Byers, John Eric
Newfield, New York
19, 106, 192, 354

Caboth, Cale D.
Mt. Pleasant, Iowa
244

Campbell, Graham
Smithville, Tennessee
160, 205, 212, 394

Chalfant, Derek Lance
Elmira, New York
314

Chandler, Nicholas
Seville, Spain
37

Clark, John
Penland, North Carolina
127, 296

Clayton, Keith Kaar
Chicago, Illinois
186

Clinch, Andrew
Seattle, Washington
27, 378

Cobb, Charles B.
Santa Rosa, California
140, 201

Colwell, David
Llawryglyn, Powys, Wales
59, 284

Condran, Brian M.
Martinez, California
282

Cook, Chanin
Napa, California
236

Costa, Jennifer
East Peoria, Illinois
207

Cottingham, Walt
Zirconia, North Carolina
401

Cox, Fletcher
Tougaloo, Mississippi
326

Cox, Jeremy J.
Philadelphia, Pennsylvania
21, 23, 118, 120

Crosby, Wesley A.
Savannah, Georgia
362

Cullen, Michael
Petaluma, California
32, 92

d'Epagnier, Arnold
Silver Spring, Maryland
171

Davis, Derek Secor
Boulder, Colorado
12, 202

de Forest, Michael
Portland, Oregon
384

Dehner, Justin
Savannah, Georgia
159

Del Guidice, Mark
Norwood, Massachusetts
111, 124

Dell, Irve W.
Minneapolis, Minnesota
66

Delp, Jon
Chantilly, Virginia
199

Diemoz, Frances M.
Santa Fe, New Mexico
392

Doerder, Aaron M.
Carbondale, Illinois
211, 304

Dougherty, Patrick L.
Bellevue, Kentucky
411

Drake, Oliver
Bristol, United Kingdom
109

ducduc
New York, New York
53

Dunn, Asher N.
Pawtucket, Rhode Island
109

During, Stefan
Oosterend, Texel, Holland
311

Edie, Jonathan
Napa, California
271, 314

Edwards, Ken
Palo Alto, California
105

Epstein, Miles
San Francisco, California
116

Erasmus, Neil
Perth, Australia
102

Eriksmoen, Ashley Jameson
Oakland, California
341

Ernst, Karen
Edinboro, Pennsylvania
93

Fanning, Douglas E.
New York, New York
50, 378

Fedarko, Aaron C.
Camden, Maine
278

Ferrell, Brian
Greensburg, Pennsylvania
357, 359

Fieber, Leonard
Manistique, Michigan
190, 323

Fiegl, Tracy A.
Fillmore, New York
263, 351

Fireman, Brian
Tryon, North Carolina
181

Fisher, Adam D.
Stony Brook, New York
364

Fleming, Shaun
Haiku, Hawaii
219

Fobes, David
San Diego, California
337, 385

Foehl, Mark C.
Wyomissing, Pennsylvania
196

Fogelvik, Mats
Makawao, Hawaii
391

Fortune, Michael C.
Lakefield, Ontario, Canada
16, 31, 72, 165

Fraser, David C.
Nelson, British Columbia, Canada
347

Freeman, Keaton
Frederick, Maryland
128

French, Adrian, B.
Hamburg, Pennsylvania
69

Furlani, Kerry O.
Rutland, Vermont
35, 45

Furrer, Stefan
Fort Bragg, California
100, 308

Galenza, Gordon
Calgary, Alberta, Canada
217, 257

Gehner, Greg
Edinboro, Pennsylvania
231, 254

Gerner, Anton
Hawthorn East, Victoria, Australia
96

Geske, Alexandra
Indianapolis, Indiana
198, 235

Gilliland, Matthew Michael
Waukegan, Illinois
56

Gilmartin, Michael J.
Atlanta, Georgia
64, 208

Glass, Genya
Richmond, Virginia
254

Gloor, Michael
Peace Dale, Rhode Island
28, 240, 315

Godfrey, John M.
Belvidere, New Jersey
98

Godfried, Lawrence
New York, New York
168

Gompf, Floyd
Lakeside, Michigan
3, 97, 312

Gowdy, Duncan W.
Worcester, Massachusetts
286

Granzow, Gwen H.
Milwaukee, Wisconsin
324

Green, Christopher
Seattle, Washington
321

Green, Don
Delhi, New York
141, 342, 360, 372

Greenwood, David
Grand Rapids, Michigan
47

Gregorio, Michael A.
Rhinebeck, New York
39, 149

Grew-Sheridan, Carolyn
San Francisco, California
303

Griffith, Robert A.
Hallstead, Pennsylvania
48, 287

Grove, Scott
Rochester, New York
39, 365

Guarino, Glen
Cedar Grove, New Jersey
132, 267

Guérin, Kino
Quebec, Canada
17, 30

Haig, David
Nelson, New Zealand
125

Hale, Naushon
Duxbury, Massachusetts
221

Hare, Rob
Ulster Park, New York
389

Hawk, Adam
Carbondale, Illinois
304

Hebert, Matthew G.
San Diego, California
179

Heck, Bailey Humbert
Brooklyn, New York
150, 234, 319

Heitzman, Roger
Scotts Valley, California
335, 402

Helmkamp, Robb
Asheville, North Carolina
288

Hergesheimer, Dave
Thousand Oaks, California
113

Heydinger, Charles F.
Sandusky, Ohio
259

Hirsh, Logan
Carbondale, Illinois
230

Hjorth-Westh, Ejler
Elk, California
295, 329

Hogbin, Stephen
Lake Charles, Canada
82, 84, 146

Holman, Steve
Dorset, Vermont
77

Holzer, Hank
Seattle, Washington
264

Houck, John
Los Angeles, California
273

Hubel, Brian A.
Colorado Springs, Colorado
139, 170

Hucker, Thomas
Hoboken, New Jersey
232

Huling, Jan
Hoboken, New Jersey
410

Hurwitz, David
Randolph, Vermont
35, 45, 252, 274

Hutton, Matt T.
Portland, Maine
260, 339

Irving, Joan
Escondido, California
251, 317

Jacquard, Nicole
Bloomington, Indiana
143, 204

Johns, Brad
San Diego, California
258

Johnson, Jeff
Poughkeepsie, New York
286

Judd, Richard
Paoli, Wisconsin
17, 305, 349

Kamerath, Danny
Dallas, Texas
244, 271

Kenway, Tony David
Coorabell, Australia
277, 330

Kim, Myung Rye
Baltimore, Maryland
42

Koons, Mark Alan
Wheatland, Wyoming
123

Kopp, Andrew Aaron
Solon, Iowa
373

Krivoshein, Mervyn L.
Rocky Mountain House,
Alberta, Canada
164

Kulin, Jacob M.
Boston, Massachusetts
151, 397

Kwon, Yang-Jun
San Diego, California
145, 225

Laberge, William
Dorset, Vermont
94

Lastomirsky, Joe
Portland, Oregon
71, 206, 399

Leake, Gary A.
Coupeville, Washington
132

Leelavoravong, Wuthichai
Bangkok, Thailand
285

Leong, Po Shun
Winnetka, California
61, 130, 163, 371

Lepo
Lima, Ohio
85

Levin, Mark S.
San Jose, New Mexico
129, 183, 241

Levine, Aaron
Bainbridge Island, Washington
36, 360

Levy, Burt
Prescott, Wisconsin
135, 294, 297

Lewis, Dale
Oneonta, Alabama
34, 90, 177, 203

Liberman, Yoav S.
Cambridge, Massachusetts
164, 388

Lifland, Kerin
Los Angeles, California
298

Loh, Peter
Bellevue, Washington
86, 200, 290

Lott, Ted
Gatlinburg, Tennessee
306

Lunin, David J.
Lancaster, Pennsylvania
261

Lynch, Paul
Woodland, California
262, 302

Macdonald, Andrew S.
De Soto, Illinois
325

Maddox, Timothy
Asheville, North Carolina
43

Makepeace, John
Dorset, England
87

Mann, Phillip
Providence, Rhode Island
76

Marsh, Bob
Grand Rapids, Michigan
51, 157, 191, 366

Martell, Michael
Akron, Ohio
187, 355

Martin, Chris
Ames, Iowa
22, 239

Martin, Katherine L.
Kalamazoo, Michigan
154, 210

Mason, Wells
Coupland, Texas
14

Matysek-Snyder, Heath
Madison, Wisconsin
26, 103

McBrien, Mason B.
Rockport, Maine
197

McDermott, John
Asheville, North Carolina
59, 248, 255

McIntyre, Damon
Richmond, Virginia
405

McLennan, Alison J.
Oakland, California
215, 216, 237

McNabb, James P.
Montville, New Jersey
89

McNew, Ryan E.
Indianapolis, Indiana
175

Melia, John-Paul
Hebden Bridge, England
112

Mercado, Rosario
San Diego, California
380

Metcalf, Josh
Pomfret, Vermont
94

Minier, Curt
Vashon, Washington
303, 382

Minniti, Paul M.
Rochester, New York
188, 333

Monahan, Thomas J.
Cedar Rapids, Iowa
351

Montgomery, Hugh N.
Bainbridge Island, Washington
334, 352

Morel, John E.
Dewinton, Alberta, Canada
247, 334

Morrow, Melissa
Toronto, Ontario, Canada
195

Morrow, Pat
Evergreen, Colorado
185, 266

Moss, Donald H.
West Hartford, Connecticut
131, 344

Mujtaba, Sabiha
Clarkston, Georgia
180, 184, 350

Mullenbach, Steve
Mapleview, Minnesota
42, 252

Nelson, Brad Reed
Carbondale, Colorado
259, 280, 281

Niswonger, Bart
Holyoke, Massachusetts
40, 41

Nutt, Craig
Kingston Springs, Tennessee
124, 142, 299, 398

O'Leary, Catherine M.
East Malvern, Victoria, Australia
404

Oates, Christy
San Diego, California
107, 156

Oh, Sunhee
Seoul, South Korea
119

Olejnik, Monika
Oakville, Ontario, Canada
81, 373

Ortega, Katherine
San Diego, California
229, 339

Orth, David
Marengo, Illinois
318

Osborne, Benjamin R.
Roswell, Georgia
191

Osgood, Jere
Wilton, New Hampshire
101, 238, 294, 395

Ouwehand, Todd
Los Angeles, California
104, 128

Papay, Marcus C.
San Diego, California
114

Parillo, Marlene Ferrell
Lincolndale, New York
212

Park, Chulyeon
San Diego, California
52

Peteran, Gord
Toronto, Ontario, Canada
269, 301, 367, 383

Petrie, Wayne J.
Orange, New South Wales, Australia
267, 343

Plummer, Todd A.
Morgan Hill, California
54, 108

Poehlmann, Christopher
Milwaukee, Wisconsin
195, 225

Pollard, Harold R.
Klamath Falls, Oregon
57

Porembski, Alice
Redding, California
136

Potts, David
Adelaide, Australia
80

Prisco, Richard
Savannah, Georgia
63

Puksta, Frederick
Keene, New Hampshire
161, 253

Puryear, Michael
Shokan, New York
115, 144, 291

Quan, John
Athelstone, Australia
82

Randall, Dan
Carbondale, Illinois
304

Ransmeier, Joseph S.
Asheville, North Carolina
275

Rasp, Sabine Gertraud
Maidstone, Kent, England
328

Regan, Michael
Chicago, Illinois
343

Rehmar, Mark
O'Brien, Oregon
368, 382, 403

Reid, Robert G.
Frenchtown, New Jersey
365

Reynolds, Sam T.
Raleigh, North Carolina
409

Richards, Ken
Maple Valley, Washington
91

Rittenhouse, Laura
San Luis Obispo, California
70, 222

Robinson, Cory
Indianapolis, Indiana
220

Rodel, Kevin P.
Brunswick, Maine
227

Rodie, John (Jack)
York, Maine
347

Rolland, Seth
Port Townsend, Washington
88, 126, 134, 322

Romeu, Gabriel Luis
Chesterfield, New Jersey
86, 159

Rosenberger, Jerry
Crofton, Maryland
55

Rosenthal, Sylvie
Asheville, North Carolina
256, 376

Ross, Angus
Perthshire, England
265

Russell, Carol
Prescott, Arizona
237

Ryu, Taeyoul
West Henrietta, New York
29, 121

Samson, Steven T.
Grand Rapids, Michigan
11

Sargent, Brian L.
Candia, New Hampshire
232

Sawada, Masafumi
Niseko, Japan
20, 245

Schleifer, Mordechai
Hod-Hasharon, Israel
62, 406

Schlerman, Carl
Williamsburg, Massachusetts
40

Schneider, Jason
Snowmass Village, Colorado
199, 290

Schriber, James
New Milford, Connecticut
95

Schürch, Paul
Santa Barbara, California
400

Schwager, Bruce
Langley, Washington
138

Schwarz, Jennifer E.
Honaunau, Hawaii
172

Segal, Adrien Rutigliano
San Francisco, California
243

Seiler, Ryan P.
Ames, Iowa
83

Sfirri, Mark
New Hope, Pennsylvania
75, 307

Sharp, Alfred
Woodbury, Tennessee
162

Shea, Chris
Brandywine, Maryland
398

Sheridan, John Grew
San Francisco, California
187, 276

Siebeneck, Craig A.
Kalida, Ohio
182

Sigler, Douglas E.
Penland, North Carolina
158, 307, 361

Simcox, David
Frome, Somerset, England
393

Simić, Srdjan
San Diego, California
49

Simpson, Thomas R.
Monroe City, Indiana
388

Singer, Michael
Felton, California
44

Sio, Carter Jason
Newtown, Pennsylvania
169, 170, 223

Skidmore, Brent Harrison
Asheville, North Carolina
13, 242, 356, 374

Skinnell, Rush
Knoxville, Tennessee
110

Slamm, Roy Alan
South Solon, Maine
270, 331

Smith, Brad
Worcester, Pennsylvania
140, 377

Smith, Greg B.
Fort Bragg, California
208, 218

Smith, Janice C.
Philadelphia, Pennsylvania
226, 313, 396

Smith, Rick E.
Murphysboro, Illinois
353

Snook, Alexandra
Florence, Massachusetts
272

Soderbergh, Jeff
Middletown, Rhode Island
64

Stammerjohn, Carl
San Pedro, California
262

Stearns, Joe
Traverse City, Michigan
369

Sthreshley, Charles A.
Ashland, Virginia
146, 274

Sun, Chia-Wei
Kaohsiung, Taiwan
396

Szymanski, Lynn
Rollinsford, New Hampshire
289

Tatam, Lucy
Hebden Bridge, England
112

Tedrowe, Jr., R. Thomas
Columbus, Indiana
79

Tennant, Phillip
Indianapolis, Indiana
166, 246

Thibodeau, Craig
San Diego, California
174, 409

Thomas, William
Rindge, New Hampshire
73

Townsend, Travis
Lexington, Kentucky
46

Tribble, Barry W.
Marion, North Carolina
346

Trubridge, David
Havelock North, New Zealand
181, 309, 326

Upfill-Brown, David
Rockport, Maine
74, 336

Upton, Gary
Nevada City, California
340

Van Dyke, Cameron
Grand Rapids, Michigan
178

Vande Griend, Dean
Story City, Iowa
122, 363

Vaughan, Richard
Brisbane, Australia
293

Vesper, Kerry
Tempe, Arizona
33, 58

Vilkman, Jari-Pekka
Vantaa, Finland
26, 69

Volotzky, Alisha
Cornell, California
33, 381

Waddell, Kevin J.
Oxford, Mississippi
413

Wade, David O.
Orange, California
229

Wallin, Jeff
Cobden, Illinois
5, 117

Wanrooij, Paulus
Woolwich, Maine
153

Wargin, Natalie
Chicago, Illinois
345

Way, Ed
Florence, Massachusetts
272

Wedig, Dale J.
Marquette, Michigan
18, 233

Wehrens, Jan
München, Germany
49, 319

Weil, Eric
Brooklyn, New York
25, 68

Wellman, Matthew
Rochester, New York
283

Wells, William J.
Ypsilanti, Michigan
298

Whittlesey, Stephen
West Barnstable, Massachusetts
10, 137, 327, 370

Whyte, Jay
Knoxville, Tennessee
133

Wiggers, John
Whitby, Ontario, Canada
24, 98, 352

Winkle, Kimberly
Smithville, Tennessee
174, 379

Younger, Jay
Oregon City, Oregon
248

Zeber-Martell, Claudia
Akron, Ohio
187, 355

Zenone, Mark
Harpers Ferry, West Virginia
91, 375

Zercher, D. Lowell
Chugiak, Alaska
205